THE
WHISPERS
of ANGELS

Annette Smith

HARVEST HOUSE PUBLISHERS

EUGENE, OREGON

THE WHISPERS OF ANGELS
Copyright © 1998 by Annette Smith
Published 2010 by Harvest House Publishers
Eugene, Oregon 97402
www.harvesthousepublishers.com

ISBN 978-0-7369-2865-6

Library of Congress Cataloging-in-Publication Data
Smith, Annette.
    The whispers of angels / Annette Smith.
        p.   cm.
    ISBN 978-1-56507-894-9
    1. Smith, Annette.   2. Christian biography—United States.
  3. Nurses—United States—Biography.   4. Nursing—Religious
    aspects—Christianity.   I. Title.
BR1725.S48A3   1998
261.8'321'092—dc21   98-5762
[B]   CIP

Printed in the United States of America

10 11 12 13 14 15 16 17 18 / VP-SK / 10 9 8 7 6 5 4 3 2

For Randy

Acknowledgments

The writing and publishing of this book have been wonderful experiences in grace and unexpected good fortune for me. Without the support and encouragement of friends and family, it would have never come to be. I wish to thank the following folks:

- My husband, Randy, a man who thrives on routine and predictability, for supporting me, loving me, and encouraging me as I take us on yet another wild ride.
- My children, Russell and Rachel, for being my greatest blessings.
- My dad, Louie Woodall, for passing on to me the gift of storytelling.
- My mom, Marolyn Woodall, for having the courage to change and grow, and for encouraging me to do the same.
- My brother, Dayne Woodall, for lending technical support, and his wife, Martha, for insisting I call her friend who was "an agent or editor or something."
- My brother, Bruce Woodall, for encouraging me, in word and in deed, to write.
- My sister-in-love, Sara Smith, for understanding and living Romans 12:15 better than anyone I know.
- Jeanna Lambert, for being my friend for 20 years and the person with whom I always feel safe.
- My buddy Darleen Jones, for predicting the rapid success of this book. You were right!
- My mentor and friend, Mattie Lou Pillows, whose enthusiasm and energy and insider's understanding continue to add to my fun.
- Mickey Gilbert, for responding to my computer S.O.S.
- My agent, Becky Freeman, whose talent and enthusiasm are both infective and effective.
- Chip MacGregor, on whose desk my proposal was blessed to fall.
- The patients and nurses who continue to enrich my life and inspire these and other stories.

Most of all,
I wish to thank the God of heaven,
who entrusts me with the ability to see and record.
To Him be the glory!

Contents

Listen to My Heart

🐦 🐦 🐦

Part One: A Child Shall Lead Them

🐦 🐦 🐦

Part Two: Family Ties

🐦 🐦 🐦

Part Three: In Sickness and in Health

❧ ❧ ❧

Part Four: Closer Than a Brother

❧ ❧ ❧

Part Five: Lessons Learned

Because of my unique position as a nurse, I am present when people face some of the most intimate, soul-baring situations of their lives. I see them cry and I hear them laugh. I am privy to their secrets.

The stories in this book are about some of the most memorable patients and most meaningful situations I have been privileged to witness. To protect the privacy of those involved, and to weave a compelling story, names, settings, and certain details have been altered.

Although all of the stories included in this book were inspired by actual people and events, none are intended to be factual accounts of specific situations.

Listen to My Heart

So soon did I begin nursing school after my high school graduation that it seems I stepped out of my cap and gown straight into my blue-striped student nurse uniform. In reality, one week passed between the end of my childhood and the beginning of my career.

Nursing school was grueling, but I was so excited to be there that I soaked up the knowledge presented me like a surgical sponge. The curriculum included anatomy, physiology, microbiology, psychology, and nursing courses.

The first skills taught in my nursing class were those of physical examination. My classmates and I learned to perform head-to-toe assessments by practicing on each other. I learned this process and continue to use it in my work today.

Beginning at the patient's head, I assess for orientation and alertness. I palpate the neck for stiffness or enlarged nodes, then listen to the chest. Moving to the abdomen, I feel for tenderness or masses and listen for bowel sounds. Finally I check reflexes and palpate the feet for pulses.

A nursing assessment is not unpleasant for the patient or for the nurse. Generally no pain is involved and it gives the nurse and patient a chance to communicate with each other without interruption.

Though patients are interested in all of my notations, I have discovered that one finding is of greatest concern to almost every one of them. During my assessment (or maybe after I have completed it) they ask:

"Nurse, can you listen to my heart?"

I respond to them by warming my stethoscope in my palm and gently placing it on their chest. Their breathing slows and their bodies relax a bit. I listen intently for almost a full minute. Sometimes I hear rapid beats, slow beats, or irregularities. Occasionally I hear the characteristic "click" of a mechanical heart valve or the "swoosh" of a murmur.

These sounds always mean something. They are important and I make careful note of them.

Yet there is much more for me to hear in these sounds of my patients' hearts. If I remain *still* enough and *quiet* enough, and listen *carefully* enough and *long* enough to my patients, I can hear different kinds of sounds. I hear my patients' stories, the stories of their hearts.

These stories always mean something important. I listen to them carefully, and I will treasure them for years to come.

PART ONE

A Child Shall Lead Them

CHAPTER ONE

Just a Push

*O*ften the scenes I witness while working as a nurse affect how I care for my family. Observing the injuries inflicted by car accidents has made me somewhat of a crusader for the use of seat belts. Because I have seen numerous cases of skin cancer, I insist that my family apply sunscreen. I keep tabs on my husband's blood pressure because I've treated men his age with serious heart disease. I can't seem to always leave my "nurse's hat" at the hospital, and occasionally I take things a bit too far.

❧ ❧ ❧

I like to think that a busy hospital emergency room is not so different from the produce section in a large supermarket. Just as a supermarket offers items of seasonal abundance—strawberries in the spring, watermelons in the summer, pumpkins in the fall, and sweet potatoes all winter—the same could be said of an emergency room. Football injuries abound in the fall; fractured, "slipped on the ice" bones in the winter; allergies in the spring; and in the summer, sunburns, bug bites, poison ivy rashes, and the most dreaded seasonal incident of all—lawnmower accidents.

The variety and severity of the injuries that power lawn-mowers inflict is amazing. The number of unwise and down-right foolish things that folks do with lawnmowers to get themselves hurt is surprising.

People operate their mowers barefoot or wearing only flimsy sandals, and then mow right over their feet. In a hurry, they zoom over rocks and gravel and end up with assorted painful debris embedded in their eyes. They even slice their fingers while trying to dislodge items interfering with the cut-ting blades while their machines are still running.

Almost in a league of their own are the mechanically gifted yardmen. These fellows dramatically increase their chances of injury by disengaging the pesky safety mechanisms built into new mowers as soon as they get them home from the store.

Injuries from lawnmower accidents can range from minor cuts and scrapes requiring bandages and tetanus shots to amputated toes requiring emergency surgery. But no matter what the severity of any particular injury, I remain convinced that *these are dangerous machines*. They should be operated by cautious adults using proper safety equipment.

Rarely have I been accused of being an overly protective mother. To the contrary, I've endured my share of surprised looks and pointed comments as my children embarked on more than a few slightly unusual, possibly precarious, parent-condoned adventures.

However, even if this time I *was* considered to be overly protective, I wouldn't budge in my decision. My six-year-old daughter, Rachel, would not be allowed to drive the riding mower while we spent the weekend at her grandparents' house. It didn't matter to me that the blade was turned off or that the gears were set low. Lawnmowers are not toys. She could not drive it.

My parental popularity did not increase when her husky, same-aged cousin Tyler *was* allowed to drive the mower. Around and around the yard Tyler drove, albeit at a pace slow enough to shame a snail, head high, back straight, carefully steering the mighty motorized machine. Rachel sat glumly on the porch, chin in hands. Tyler waved tauntingly toward her at every turn.

I stood by the window and watched them for a few minutes, then turned my attention to coffee and conversation with my mother and Tyler's more lenient mom, Martha. In a half-hour or so I stole another peek.

I was shocked and angered to see, in the distance, my Rachel perched on the slow-moving mower, smiling and waving like a queen on a coronation float as she steered up the steep hill toward the house. Tyler was nowhere to be seen.

She had *deliberately* disobeyed me.

It had no doubt been *Tyler's* idea.

I stormed out the door, set to pull her right off that machine. But I was surprised to hear curious silence rather than the loud roar of the mower. I trotted across the yard toward Rachel and realized the engine wasn't running. Still, the machine, with my daughter precariously perched in the seat, inched up the steep hill. Finally, when I reached her, I saw behind the mower, red-faced, sweating, and almost bent to the ground, her adoring and easily charmed cousin. Rachel was riding the mower all right, steering it herself and everything, but Tyler was providing every bit of the horsepower. He was pushing the heavy lawnmower, with her on it, inch by strenuous inch.

Tyler had come up with a way for Rachel to get to drive the lawnmower and hopefully avoid getting into trouble. Her look of pure joy was dimmed only by the look of obvious pride on his flushed face. Tyler figured right—no one got into any trouble at all.

Sometimes I find it enjoyable to be in an enviable position, the recipient of a coveted assignment, the person chosen to participate in some rare opportunity. I bask in the attention, the momentary praise and notoriety. But quickly, so very quickly, that position becomes a lonely one.

Being in the driver's seat while everyone else watches from the porch isn't fun for very long. The enjoyment of waving at every turn quickly becomes stale and the folks on the porch don't always wave back.

I think my nephew Tyler has the right idea: He knows that after a spin or two around the yard, it's usually best to get in the back, do a little pushing, and let someone else have a turn at the wheel.

Don't let anyone look down on you because you are young, but set an example for the believers.

—1 TIMOTHY 4:12

CHAPTER TWO

A Story of Hope

A nurse is often used as a consultant, called upon to make necessary recommendations to adapt situations and environments for people with disabilities. That was the situation I found myself in when I observed a rowdy P.E. class and their response to a new student.

℘ ℘ ℘

Hope greets Coach with a big "Hi" and a confident smile. It is the first day of school after the Christmas holidays and Hope's first day at Beaver Elementary School. Ten years old, she moved to Beaver with her mom and dad the last week of December.

Today is a big day for Hope. It's her first try at public school, because her previous academic achievements have been at the state school for the blind. Beaver is a small community and there is no special school. Students with all types of needs and challenges are integrated into the local public system. Often a nurse works with the child's teacher to provide assistance with any special problems that may come up.

Anyway, that's how Hope happens to be standing in front of Coach and the combined third, fourth, and fifth-grade P.E.

classes, and how I happen to be observing this preadolescent drama. Eighty-three wriggly, opinionated, sock-footed athletes stand in their assigned spots on the gritty gym floor ready to assess the new kid and to watch Coach's response to her.

Coach's main assignment is coaching the varsity football team. Football is his love and his talent, but in this small school, all faculty members have at least two duties. Mrs. Wood, the principal's secretary, doubles as the school's librarian, and Mr. Jones, who works in the cafeteria, is responsible for changing lightbulbs and stocking toilet paper in the restrooms.

The way Coach sees it, teaching elementary students the finer points of jumping jacks and dodgeball isn't such a bad assignment, and he likes doing it.

To keep a measured level of controlled chaos in his P.E. classes, Coach has developed some essential strategies and rules. Everyone has an assigned place on the gym floor. Each student uses the various lanes, boundaries, and markings painted on the gym floor to find his or her place. Though not exactly hallowed ground, the wood floor does scuff easily, so the first order of the day is for each student to remove his shoes and go directly to his or her assigned place.

Coach first checks roll. After that he leads his squirmy charges in calisthenics. He insists that the students do enough toe touches and leg lunges to break a sweat and burn off the excess energy that has built up during a morning spent learning math, reading, and social studies. The last portion of the period is spent in games or drills.

Coach also has rules like No Cussing, No Spitting on Your Neighbor, and Always Wear Socks, but everyone knows that the most important rule is Go to Your Own Place.

So here stands Hope. Someone has told her about the Take Off Your Shoes rule, so she holds her purple high-tops in one hand and her white folding cane in the other.

For once, Coach doesn't have to tell everyone to get quiet. Even the third-grade boys in the back row are staring, slack-jawed, to see what Coach will do about Hope. Prissy fifth-grade girls look Hope up and down and find her outfit and hairstyle acceptable. Yet everyone knows about the Get in Your Own Place rule and figures Coach will tell Hope to put her shoes back on and someone will have to take her to the office to get her schedule changed to study hall or something.

Coach looks at Hope, pulls off his cap, and scratches his head. He takes Hope by the hand and guides her to the side of the gym.

"Put the end of your cane here. This is the bottom row of bleachers. Walk straight ahead and keep your cane against the bleacher. When you get to this crack where the next section begins, stop, turn left, walk ten steps, and you'll be right in your place. Every day this is where you must be when class begins. Do you understand, Hope?"

"Yes, sir," she answers without hesitation.

"Now let's go back to where you came in, and you show me that you can find your place." Coach takes her back to where she started.

The whole class holds its collective breath as Hope faces Coach's ultimate test.

Hope taps her cane against the bleacher and slowly takes a step forward. So far so good. She takes four more steps, using her cane to guide her position.

Tap . . . tap . . . tap . . . She stops when her cane catches on something. Thinking she's reached the crack, she starts to turn left.

"Not yet!" she hears from over her right shoulder.

Hope stops and bends down to feel that the cane has caught—not on the crack she's supposed to find, but on a metal bolt. She straightens, repositions her cane, and takes three more steps before coming to the crack. This time there's no mistake, and she turns left, walks ten slow, careful steps, and stops. Hope is in Her Place.

For a moment, no one moves. Then, as if by spontaneous combustion, the whole gym bursts into cheers and clapping. The rafters shake and Mr. Peabody comes out of the janitor's closet to see what the commotion is all about.

Hope smiles.

Coach is my friend. He says we're all pretty much alike. We don't ponder many tough questions and problems. We really don't require a lot. We just need to find our place. We need a few landmarks and someone to tell us when we turn too soon. We need to know how many steps to take, when to stop, and when to take off our shoes. Most of all, we need someone to cheer for us when we finally find our place.

Coach says we really just need Hope.

Where the paths meet, she takes her stand.

—PROVERBS 8:2

CHAPTER THREE

Uphill Climb

*P*remature babies call upon a nurse's most astute assessment and treatment skills. While the course of a disease in an adult can be sometimes predicted, these tiny babies are so fragile and there are so many variables to consider that it is impossible to say what their outcomes will be. Baby Wesley's parents, however, believed from the beginning, that their son could make the uphill climb to survival.

❧ ❧ ❧

Travis and Joanne were thrilled when they learned that after four years of infertility tests and treatments, they were finally pregnant. Joanne gave up her beloved gourmet coffee, joined an exercise class for expectant mothers, and sewed yellow checked curtains for the nursery. Travis researched child safety seats, assembled the crib and changing table, and dutifully scanned the rotating stack of child-rearing books that mysteriously appeared on his nightstand.

Joanne's grandmother warned her not to raise her arms over her head, her best friend advised her not to sleep on her back, and her doctor told her not to worry. Travis' uncle told him to spoil Joanne with anything she wanted, his cousin told him to take a vacation while he still could, and the guys at the gym just shook their heads.

No one told Travis and Joanne what to do if their baby came early.

Six weeks before her due date, Joanne's back began to ache. She had spent the morning in the garden and at first thought she had just been on her feet too long. She tried to ignore the discomfort, but it only got worse. She lay down with a heating pad on her back, but felt panic rising inside her when the pain moved to her lower abdomen. Travis called Joanne's doctor, and at his urging they made the anxious trip to the hospital.

Dr. Brooks was waiting for them. His words were calm and reassuring as he examined Joanne, but he was unable to deny his alarm at what he determined to be premature labor. He had Joanne admitted, then ordered an internal fetal monitor and intravenous medication to stop the contractions.

Things seemed to be going well. The contractions stopped and Joanne dozed. Travis slumped in a vinyl chair beside her bed. Both sets of prospective grandparents paced and prayed in the waiting room.

Travis and Joanne's calm ended abruptly when, two hours after their arrival at the hospital, her water broke and the contractions returned. The rupture of membranes represents a time of "no turning back" in the birth process. Dr. Brooks was called, and within minutes Joanne was in surgery. A tiny boy, quickly named Wesley, was delivered by cesarean section. He was immediately whisked to the Neonatal Intensive Care Unit, the NICU.

At three pounds, six ounces, Wesley was not nearly the smallest baby in the NICU, but he was definitely one of the sickest. Birth weight is one of the predictors of a premature baby's outcome, but it's not the only one. Wesley's lungs were not fully developed, and his doctors, neonatologists specializing in the care of premature babies, detected both heart and intestinal problems.

Because of the surgical delivery of Wesley, Joanne was not able to come to the NICU for several hours. Travis spent his time racing between his wife's side and the closed doors of the NICU. He was given periodic reports about his son's condition, but was unable to see Wesley while efforts were made to stabilize him.

Late in the evening on the day of Wesley's birth, a day that had seemed to last a year, Travis wheeled Joanne down to the NICU and they saw their son for the first time. Connected to so many tubes and wires, his tiny eyes covered, he looked more like a baby bird dropped too early out of its nest than the rosy-cheeked child they had expected.

Day and night seem one and the same in the windowless NICU. For two weeks Travis and Joanne knew only dark nights in their souls. Wesley was so sick that no light could penetrate their sad and fearful hearts. The doctors were careful to avoid any positive predictions, but Joanne and Travis clung to every encouraging word or phrase. It is just too soon, they were told, to know if Wesley will make it.

Every hour will be an *uphill struggle*.

The NICU allows extended visiting hours, and parents may sit near their babies' cribs so long as there are no crises or procedures to be done. Joanne was able to stay at the hospital continuously, catching naps in a hospital room reserved for mothers of babies in NICU. Travis, however, had to return to work within a week.

While Joanne stayed by Wesley's side all day, Travis spent time there early every morning, again every evening, and all day on Saturday and Sunday.

Travis and Joanne talked in soothing tones to Wesley.

"How's Daddy's little man today?"

"Time to wake up, sleepyhead."

They stroked his tiny hands and feet. His grandmother made him a little teddy bear. They named the bear Bobby and propped him up in Wesley's crib. Joanne sang Disney tunes to him, and Travis, though definitely not a gifted vocalist, hummed along.

After two weeks Wesley began to show small signs of improvement. The doctors began to express cautious optimism but there were still days of setbacks and problems. Wesley's survival would still be an "uphill journey," they were repeatedly reminded.

One Saturday morning, after a particularly precarious Friday night, Travis entered the NICU, took his usual place next to Wesley's crib, and began to read to him from a storybook. All day that Saturday and several times a day from then on, Travis could be heard reading aloud from the book. During the days when Travis was at work, Joanne read the same storybook, again and again. Over and over, the words from the book fell softly on Wesley's ears, and on the ears of anyone close enough to hear them.

Wesley began to get better. A lot better.

Every day he grew a little bigger and a bit stronger. The doctors relaxed, and some even began to smile when they gave Travis and Joanne Wesley's daily progress reports. Soon Wesley's parents were able to hold him in their arms as they read from the well-worn storybook.

Finally, when he was 2½ months old, Wesley was well enough to go home. On the day of his discharge, Travis and Joanne sent an arrangement of balloons and flowers to the nurses' lounge. They also left the well-worn storybook in the NICU.

Now, even though Wesley has gone home, nurses continue to hear the words from the special book read over and over each day. The tattered volume is passed around and read by almost every parent who has a very sick baby. The familiar words that are heard so often are from *The Little Engine That Could*.

I always think of Wesley when I hear them spoken: *"I think I can . . . I think I can. . . ."*

I prayed for this child,
and the LORD has granted me what I asked of him.

—1 SAMUEL 1:27

CHAPTER FOUR

Looking for Love in All the Wrong Places

After working for years in a hospital, I relished my new position as an office nurse in a doctor's outpatient clinic, for it gave me a welcome change of scenery as well as the opportunity to observe a wide variety of generally nonurgent conditions and ailments. It was in this setting that I met a charming little boy named Scott.

❧ ❧ ❧

Scott was what the old wives call a "*good* baby." It bothered his mother, Ruth, to hear those words used to describe her child's sunny disposition.

"As opposed to what?" she wondered aloud. "A *bad* baby?"

Still, she knew what people meant. From the time of his birth, Scott had behaved as if everything that went on around him was planned solely for his enjoyment. He ate well and rarely spit up. When he was two weeks old he started sleeping through the night and never looked back. He loved to ride in the car and was content in his playpen.

Ruth's friends, exhausted from caring for their own colicky, crying infants, warned her bitterly to *just wait* until her next baby came along. *No mother,* they predicted, could expect to give birth to *two* babies as mellow as Scott.

Ruth was sympathetic toward her friends' sleepless situations, but nothing they said could keep her from totally enjoying her son. He was an affectionate, cuddly boy, and she loved to feel his chubby arms around her neck and to taste his sweet baby kisses. She thought to herself, *He is the perfect baby.*

Perfection is usually an illusion, and Ruth was caught by surprise when, at three months of age, her flawless child developed what the old wives deemed to be a *serious* behavior problem. *Scott began to suck his thumb.*

Their advice was swift and sure.

"Put socks on his hands."

"Dip his thumb in hot pepper sauce."

"Wrap masking tape around his thumb and forefinger."

"The problem *must* be stopped before it becomes a habit," was the unanimous concerned consensus.

Ruth dutifully gave each of their suggestions a halfhearted try—with the exception of the hot pepper instruction. But it didn't matter what measures she took—Scott repeatedly found ways to get to his beloved thumb.

Finally Ruth gave up and assumed her demoted position as the mother of a less-than-perfect, thumb-sucking, future-crooked-toothed baby. Admitting defeat was a relief both for her and for Scott. Ruth secretly thought he looked adorable clutching his blanket and smacking on his thumb.

Somehow, despite the grave warnings of the old wives, baby Scott grew into a sturdy three-year-old toddler. He learned to ride his red tricycle, to pick up his toys, and to count to five. Even as he became increasingly independent, he remained an affectionate, easygoing child.

There was only one problem: Scott *still* sucked his thumb—though now only when he found something to "love" on.

When this happened, he would madly clutch whatever the object might be—a blanket, a stuffed animal, even the fur collar on his mother's winter coat, hold it against his ear, and lapse into thumb-sucking ecstasy.

By this time even Ruth grew concerned. She talked to Scott. She reasoned with Scott. She even tried bribing Scott. He would look up at her with wide, unblinking eyes and solemnly tell her he would not do it *any*more. He *really* meant to keep his promises, but always, at the very next opportunity, Ruth would find him holding some beloved object against his cheek, and once again, blissfully, almost unconsciously enjoying his forbidden thumb.

Ruth came up with a new plan. Since soft objects seemed to trigger Scott's undesirable behavior, she would simply remove them from his environment. She packed up his stuffed animals, stored the family's blankets on the very highest shelves in the linen closet, and stashed her fur-collared coat in the cedar chest at the foot of her bed.

After the first day, Ruth was simply amazed at how well her plan had worked. Scott didn't even seem to miss his thumb. With no soft items around to "love" on, he seemed to lose interest in the forbidden habit. She was thrilled when he went first one week, then two, without once sucking his thumb.

The situation was well under control until Lady, the family's beloved German shepherd, had her puppies. They were truly adorable, with their soft brown-and-black fur, cute little waggly tails, and cold pink noses.

The problem was that they were soft and small and *very* lovable. Ruth tried to keep a straight face when she found Scott holding a puppy against his cheek. She tried to scold him, but the sight of the tiny boy struggling to keep a squirmy puppy up on his shoulder using only one hand—the other being in his mouth—was just too funny. Ruth did what any mother concerned about the development of her child's character would do: She grabbed the video camera.

Luckily, within a few weeks the puppies grew too heavy and wiggly for Scott to hold, and the problem solved itself.

While working as an office nurse for a physician specializing in family medicine, I observed many unusual illnesses and injuries. A new situation, however, was brought to our attention—one I had never dealt with before. Joan, the clinic's receptionist, informed me that a mother was bringing in her child who had been bitten by a *snapping turtle*—on the *cheek*.

How, I wondered, *does a turtle bite someone on the face?*

It turns out the patient was a wet-eyed, red-faced Scott. His cheek was fine, but his feelings were *very* hurt.

I asked him what happened.

He didn't know.

Had he been trying to "love" on the turtle?

Yes. Just a little. It had *looked* like such a *nice* turtle.

My friend Scott is in good company. Who among us hasn't been snapped at by someone surprisingly unappreciative of our loving offerings? Haven't we all had our feelings hurt when our best intentions were misunderstood or even rebuffed? And though we don't usually wear the scars of our affectionate attempts on our cheeks, we definitely carry them in our hearts.

Somehow, though, we recover our courage and try again. Because as critters of the warm-blooded and warmhearted variety, we *need* love.

Scott was no different.

Less than a month after the ill-tempered snapping turtle incident his mother brought him back to the clinic. This time a classmate had pushed him off the steps at preschool. He had fallen and had received a nasty gash on his left arm.

I asked Scott what had happened.

He sniffled. There was this girl. She was nice . . . he had only been trying to "love" on her . . . .

Perfect love drives out fear.

—1 John 4:18

CHAPTER FIVE

Baby Rowdy

W hen I met Sharon and Ray, I was first struck by their poverty and their lack of education. As I spent more time with them, I was impressed by their devotion to each other, by the depth of their loss, and by their simple acceptance of life's difficulties.

❧ ❧ ❧

It was just past noon when my friend Jane, working in labor and delivery, called to give me information about a transfer to my unit. The patient was a woman who less than an hour before had given birth to a premature, stillborn baby boy. Rather than assigning her a room on the obstetrical unit, where new mothers would be enjoying their healthy babies, Jane thought it best to move her upstairs to a private room on the medical-surgical unit where I was working. I agreed and quickly prepared a room for her.

My new patient's name was Sharon and she was 43 years old. Her husband, Ray, accompanied her. It was he who helped me ease her from the stretcher to the bed, and it was he who tucked an extra blanket around her trembling shoulders.

Sharon and Ray had the familiar, tired look of folks who have not had an easy time of life. His mechanic's hands were grease-stained and calloused, and an open cigarette package bulged from his torn shirt pocket. Sharon's blonde hair was clean but marred by dark roots, and her teeth were badly in need of repair. The two spoke softly, voicing their needs and requests almost apologetically. Their grammar was poor, and though I was obviously years younger than they were, they repeatedly addressed me as ma'am.

I learned that this was the second marriage for both of them and that this pregnancy had been Sharon's third. Though she had two grown daughters from her first marriage, Ray had no children of his own. Since Sharon had been told she could no longer conceive, they had been shocked to learn she was pregnant. She told me of receiving the incredible news while she was working at her convenience store job. When the nurse on the phone told her she was pregnant, she sat right down on the floor. She laughed, then she cried, then she laughed some more. Her reaction so rattled the store's 20-year-old manager that he phoned Ray at work and told him he had best come see about his wife.

In the two short years Ray and Sharon had been married, the subject of children had really never come up. At this stage of their lives, and with Sharon's supposed infertility, the couple had neither expected nor desired children. If someone had asked them about having a baby they would have laughed and explained that they didn't have the time or the money for kids. Sharon would have voiced great relief to finally have her two girls grown and raised.

But predictably, upon learning of the pregnancy, all that changed. They were so excited and talkative that friends and coworkers assumed Ray and Sharon had planned on having a baby all along. Ray behaved like any nervous first-time father-to-be would. He stopped smoking inside their mobile home and insisted that Sharon drink milk with every meal. His unexpected enthusiasm was infectious, and Sharon found

herself wearing with great pride the corny maternity T-shirt
he had bought her.

When she was five months into the pregnancy, a doctor's
office sonogram showed the baby to be a boy, and Ray's
cheers were heard down the hall. They decided to name the
baby Ray Jr. but to call him Rowdy. It would be a fitting name
for a boy they were sure would be active, strong, and most
definitely spoiled rotten.

Sharon was tremulous and teary, pale-faced and red-eyed.
Ray was shaken and badly in need of a smoke. I told him I
would stay with his wife while he stepped out for a moment.
He was both hesitant and grateful when Sharon insisted he
go. I monitored her vital signs and checked her for bleeding.
Then I helped her into a clean gown and brought her some
juice.

After she was settled and Ray had returned, I gently
asked if she had seen the baby. She had not, had assumed she
couldn't, and was touchingly grateful when I told her I could
arrange it. I looked questioningly at Ray. He stammered and
stuttered before apologetically telling Sharon he just did not
believe he could bear the sad sight of his lifeless son. She told
him she understood, they kissed, and I showed him to the visitor's waiting room.

After a few minutes of searching, I located a rocking
chair in an unoccupied pediatric room. At my request, an
orderly moved it into Sharon's room. After helping her to the
chair and draping a blanket around her shoulders, I called
Jane in obstetrics and asked her to bring the baby up.

In a few minutes we heard a soft knock at the door. I met
my friend and carefully took the child in my hands. He was
tiny and felt almost weightless in the soft blue blanket in
which she had wrapped him. I soundlessly crossed the room
and placed him in Sharon's waiting arms.

She gathered the baby to her chest and held him there
for a long moment, slowly rocking back and forth. Then she
lowered the fragile bundle, lifted the blanket from his face,

and touched his paper-thin cheek. She stroked his tiny hand and caressed his little foot.

I sat near her, my chair pulled so close that our knees touched. I listened as she admitted how upset she had been the day she found out about the pregnancy, how guilty that had made her feel, and how her feelings had changed as the baby had grown inside her. She told how she had begun to love the infant in her womb, to feel fiercely protective of it, to long to see it.

I stroked her back and spoke soft words of understanding, and when she was ready, as ready as she would ever be, I took the baby from her.

I confess I don't spend many hours contemplating heaven. I certainly look forward to being there, but with the ease and contentment I enjoy in my earthly life, I admit I don't often feel an urgent longing to go there.

The day baby Rowdy died, however, I realized for the first time a deeper understanding of the allure of heaven. I now believe that for those people who have *possessed the least* and for those who have *lost the most*, heaven will indeed be a *most special place*. For the grease-stained mechanics and the exhausted convenience store clerks, for the folks who suffer with bad teeth and the ones who speak in soft apologetic voices, for the 40-year-old couples who live together in cramped mobile homes, the promised rest of heaven will be the most welcome of all.

My heart tells me that for those who have *lost what they have loved the most*, for the Sharons and the Rays of this world, the rewards of heaven may be the sweetest of all.

Blessed are the poor in spirit,
for theirs is the kingdom of heaven.

—MATTHEW 5:3

CHAPTER SIX

Coveting a Cardboard Crown

I learned about growth and development and studied adolescent psychology in nursing school. The knowledge I gained through my study is useful to me in my work and in my daily life. My friend Sarah's daughter struggled with the confusion common to young women. I tried to offer her some advice and comfort.

♥ ♥ ♥

My neighbor and friend Sarah considers herself to be a semiliberated, mostly content, stay-at-home mom. She has been known to canvass prospective voters, change the oil in her car, and bake chocolate oatmeal cookies all in the same afternoon. She volunteers at the local battered woman's shelter, and she and her husband co-coach a soccer team. Though she has never promoted a "feminist agenda," Sarah has tried to raise her 11-year-old daughter, Shelly, to be self-confident and assertive, and to believe that she can achieve any goal she sets for herself.

One sunny Saturday, semiliberation collided head on with achievement and goal-setting. Freckle-faced, knobby-kneed

Shelly announced that her heart's desire was to compete in the Junior Miss Forest Princess beauty pageant.

Sarah squirmed and tried to stammer out words to explain why she didn't think entering the pageant was such a great idea. She rambled on about women being valued only for how they look—not for how smart or athletic or musical or artistic they are. She told Shelly, in long and breathless detail, that only a few years ago women couldn't vote or go to college and weren't allowed to participate in sports. About how, not so long ago, women had precious few choices and couldn't even think of becoming doctors or attorneys or astronauts.

But Shelly didn't want to be an attorney. She didn't want to be an astronaut. Shelly wanted to be a Junior Miss Forest Princess, and she wanted to wear a crown.

Sarah knew she was rambling. She didn't believe in beauty contests—detested them, in fact—but couldn't seem to make, or even find, her point. Ignoring her usual parenting finesse, she just flat out told Shelly no. *N-O.* No daughter of hers was going to compete in the Junior Miss Forest Princess beauty pageant, or any other beauty contest for that matter.

End of discussion.

Shelly responded as any self-confident, assertive, goal-directed 11-year-old girl would. She ran to her room and slammed the door shut.

Nothing more was said about the pageant until two weeks later, when Sarah drove Shelly and her friend Lacy (who also had a semiliberated, anti-beauty-pageant mother) to the daylong Forest Festival. The girls ate corn dogs and cotton candy, rode all the carnival rides twice, and strolled through the livestock exhibit barn.

At midafternoon they perched on folding chairs and enviously watched eight of their classmates parade across the flatbed trailer-turned-outdoor-runway. Within minutes, one of the voiceless participants was crowned Junior Miss Forest Princess, and it was all over.

Shelly and Lacy spent the rest of their money in the arts-and-crafts tent. They purchased elaborate, handmade contraptions built of wood and bits of hardware. The would-be Forest Princesses emerged from the tent well-armed with *potato shooters*. While the newly crowned Junior Miss Forest Princess was having her picture taken for the local paper, Shelly and Lacy were gleefully pelting unsuspecting festival goers with hefty chunks of prime Idaho spuds.

Much to the relief of their semiliberated mothers, neither girl seemed permanently scarred after being deprived of the coveted cardboard crown.

Later that fall I hired Shelly to help me rake leaves in my yard. She seemed a bit blue, and I gently probed to find out what was bothering her. She told me that she hated the fact that her chest was growing. It hurt when the dodge ball hit her during P.E. class, and some of the boys teased her about wearing a bra. As we raked, I talked to her about puberty and the changes that were happening in her body. I tried to sound matter-of-fact and positive, but Shelly would not be comforted. She insisted that she wanted her chest to be smaller.

We worked together and bagged the leaves. I complimented Shelly on her new boots. She proudly told me that she was now wearing a size seven, one size bigger than her mother wore. I commented that her feet possibly were through growing, and had probably already reached their full-grown size.

Shelly strongly disagreed. All her friends' feet were at least a size eight. She wanted her feet to grow to be at least as as big as theirs—hopefully even bigger.

I struggled not to smile. This brilliant, confused, graceful, awkward, crown-coveting, potato-shooting, precious woman-child had just told me that she wanted a smaller chest and bigger feet!

I gave her a big hug and assured her that she would grow up to be just perfect. Come to think of it—I think she already is.

I praise you because I am fearfully and
wonderfully made.

—PSALM 139:14

CHAPTER SEVEN

A Business Arrangement

*M*y husband, Randy, is a teacher and a coach. He cares as deeply for his students as I do for my patients. Though our jobs are not the same, sometimes our professional concerns do cross. Together, Randy and I became involved with, loved, and learned from his student and my patient, Jimmy.

ℐ♥ ℐ♥ ℐ♥

I first met Jimmy when he arrived to pick up our non-functioning lawnmower. My husband, Randy, called "Coach" by his high-school students, was Jimmy's fourth-period algebra teacher, and the two had made a business arrangement.

Randy and I are not handy with appliances or machines. When a new neighbor naively asked to borrow a couple of tools, we looked at each other and wondered whether he wanted the wire coat hanger, the bobby pin, or the roll of duct tape. Because of our mechanical ineptitude, we find it necessary to hire out almost all our household and automotive repairs.

Jimmy was good with his hands and excelled in the school's auto mechanics class, but his algebraic abilities were somewhat less than stellar. Randy can work the most complicated of math problems in his head, but when it comes to even simple repairs, he is decidedly "mechanically challenged."

So this was the deal: Jimmy would keep our lawnmower up and running, and Randy, by tutoring Jimmy after class, would get him through algebra, a credit he had to have in order to graduate with his class in May.

Each secretly believed he had received the better end of the bargain.

But each had taken on a bigger task than he realized.

Jimmy had to repeatedly resurrect our chronically ailing lawnmower. Over and over he would have it working just fine, but after one or two mowings it would once again refuse to start. He would show up at our house, painfully ask me if perhaps Coach had tried to work on it, look incredibly relieved when I told him no, and hoist it into the back of his elderly pickup truck, where it was beginning to look increasingly at home. In a day or two the mower would appear in our garage, returned once again to working order.

Randy also had his share of frustrations. Jimmy tried, he really did. But algebra was *extremely* hard for him, and he already had a failing average. Twice a week Randy would patiently go over and over the most difficult problems, and each Friday Jimmy would barely, just barely, pass the week's quiz. Every time he squeaked by, Randy would heave a sigh of relief and count up how many more quizzes Jimmy had to pass to get his needed math credit.

It was a long semester.

Just one month before the final algebra exam, Jimmy was involved in an accident. He was driving way too fast down a dirt road, lost control of his truck, and rolled it over twice. Miraculously, though he wasn't wearing his seat belt, he survived. He did, however, almost lose his right arm.

The compassionate and skilled surgeon on duty the night of the accident worked a medical miracle and avoided amputation. Sadly, because of great damage to the muscles and multiple shattered bones, the limb would never regain full strength or have complete range of motion. This kid was just lucky not to have lost his arm.

Ten days after having surgery, Jimmy could go home but would need daily sterile dressing changes. He had no insurance and didn't qualify for government home health benefits. I spoke with his doctor and volunteered my time, and the home health agency I was working for graciously donated the expensive bandages he would need.

The day after his discharge from the hospital, I phoned Jimmy and told him I was coming to change his dressing. I thought he seemed a bit hesitant, but he told me how to find his house. Following his directions, I drove deeper and deeper into the forest. Finally, at the end of a muddy road, I arrived at the unpainted, falling-down shack Jimmy called home. Garbage was strewn over the front porch. Two rusted-out cars and an abandoned refrigerator were the only items taller than the grass in the yard.

A barking, sniffing, mangy-looking dog announced my approach and Jimmy yelled for me to come on in. The little house was stifling hot and so poorly lit it took my eyes several minutes to adjust. Finally I could see Jimmy lying on a threadbare couch, pale-faced, sleepy, shirtless, and skinnier than I remembered him being.

"Hey, Mrs. Smith," he said as he rubbed his eyes.

"Hey, Jimmy. How are you feeling? How's your arm?"

We made small talk while I removed the bandage, cleaned his mangled arm, and applied ointment and a fresh gauze dressing. When a pesky housefly repeatedly landed on his wound, I asked, "Are you still taking antibiotics?"

"Yes, ma'am."

Relief!

Jimmy lived with his disabled dad, who I saw only once during the three weeks I made daily visits to his house. I could tell Jimmy was embarrassed by the run-down condition of the house and yard. He had frequently visited our small but mostly clean house. He told me he was the person who usually washed the dishes and swept the floor, but since his injury those tasks had simply not been done.

I offered to help but he wouldn't hear of it.

We didn't talk about algebra or lawnmowers. Those concerns seemed a long time past. Randy had long since given up on our cranky old mower and bought a dependable new one with an extended warranty. Jimmy had missed the last month of school, and of course he didn't graduate with his class. Randy was sure he wouldn't have gone on to college anyway, and besides, now he would qualify for a disability check just like his dad.

I tried not to think of his future.

I guess you could say Jimmy's arm healed. The messy wound dried and scarred. He couldn't lift his arm from the shoulder, but his elbow would bend a little and he could move his fingers enough to grasp small objects.

Once the wound closed, I told Jimmy I wouldn't need to come back. I wished him well and told him to call me if he needed anything. As I turned to leave, he stopped me.

"Mrs. Smith, I've got your lawnmower ready for you. I know you've been needing it and it's taken me a long time, but I got it done. It's running just fine."

"But, Jimmy, how did you work on the mower with your arm all bandaged up?" I was incredulous.

"I just used my good arm. It wasn't so hard. Just took twice as long. Let me know if it quits on you again. Okay?"

I drove home thinking about a kid without much going for him, a kid without many chances. I thought about a kid who would never pass algebra and would not graduate from high school.

But I also drove home thinking about a kid who kept up his end of a deal, who knew the importance of a commitment, and who perhaps had more chances and more going for him than I would ever know or understand.

I drove home with a lawnmower in perfect working order.

Rich and poor have this in common:

The LORD is the Maker of them all.

—PROVERBS 22:2

CHAPTER EIGHT

Pushing a Purple Stroller

*B*ecause of my nursing expertise, our family was given the opportunity to serve as a foster family for a newborn baby, a tiny boy not yet 24 hours old. Taking care of him, with the help of my daughter, was easy. Giving him up was not.

❧ ❧ ❧

I was making dinner when the call came. An unplanned pregnancy had, only hours before, turned into an unwanted baby. We were a licensed foster family, between placements, and a hopeful but almost frantic social worker was on the other end of the line.

I had a part-time job to go to in the morning, the kids had open house at school later in the evening, and my husband would coach a volleyball tournament on Thursday, Friday, and Saturday.

Jenny, the social worker assigned to us by the Christian foster care agency we served under, explained that she was in need of a family to care for a newborn baby. She remembered that we usually took toddlers and older children, but because

I was a nurse, and because he was so tiny, she especially wanted to place him with us.

"When?" I questioned her as I scanned the calendar. "When would the placement begin?" *Once this weekend tournament was over,* I mused, *things would settle down at our house.*

"Well—mmm—I need to pick him up from the hospital, and then I would bring him to you—oh, in about—let's say about a couple of hours."

Two hours! To prepare for a baby! I remembered how my husband and I had prepared for *months* for the arrivals of our own children. We had been given showers by our family and friends, purchased the perfect crib, and carefully arranged the nursery. I had washed, ironed, and folded tiny clothes, and together we had dreamed happy dreams about the infant who would soon arrive.

This baby would not have those important preparations made for his arrival. He would barely have any preparations made for him at all, but we would do our best. I got on the phone, and within half an hour I had rounded up a portable crib, sheets, and blankets. Our neighbors, Steve and Melanie, made a run to Wal-Mart for diapers and bottles, and my friend Judy brought over an infant car seat.

Word travels fast in suburbia, and within minutes the whole neighborhood was on high alert for the baby's arrival. I glanced up and down our street and waved at three families who stood watching from their yards as the social worker pulled into our driveway. Five elementary-school girls rode up on their bikes and gazed enviously at my daughter, Rachel, as she followed Jenny and the newborn into the house.

The baby, named Tony, weighed six pounds and two ounces. He was 23 hours old. He had curly dark hair. His skin was the color of coffee with cream.

"I knew there was something I forgot to tell you," squirmed Jenny.

I didn't care what color he was, but I admit it *was* a surprise when I lifted the blanket and first saw his scrunched-up, dark little face. He blinked lazily and began to cry.

Jenny told us just a bit about Tony's family. His parents were married and in their late twenties, and already had seven children. They were overwhelmed both financially and emotionally. Tony would be adopted and we would care for him until a family was found. The placement would be for only about two weeks.

We had been out of the baby business for so long that my husband, Randy, and I were out of practice. Tony was small but healthy. He didn't need a nurse, but it still took all of us, including our son, Russell, and daughter, Rachel, to keep Tony fed, rocked, and changed. Tony was a restless sleeper and was truly content only when nestled on a warm chest, his head snuggled under a cozy chin. We indulged him, and Randy and I slept in shifts, drowsily handing him over in the hall at four-hour intervals.

Rachel was an especially big help with Tony. Eight years old, she had been preparing for this maternal role all her short life. She always kept her dolls well-dressed and fed, and administered only the gentlest of discipline when they misbehaved. Having a *real* baby to tend to was a dream come true for her.

Tony fit perfectly into the crook of Rachel's arm. She fed him, diapered him, and bounced and burped him. She bathed him and rubbed oil into his hair. When he cried, she walked him, and when he was happy, she dressed him in cute outfits and slowly wheeled him around the house in her purple doll stroller. He seemed to love those stroller rides, and she never tired of carefully pushing him from the kitchen to the living room, to each of the three bedrooms, and back again.

After Tony had been with us for about two weeks, Jenny called. She had found an adoptive family who was thrilled at the prospect of having a new son. She would come for him on Friday.

Only Rachel and I were at home when Jenny came to get Tony to take him to his new family. She and I had packed all his things, and now we turned our efforts to trying not to cry.

Rachel asked the social worker if she could hold the baby just one more time. Jenny hesitated, saw Rachel's pleading eyes, and agreed. She carefully positioned Rachel in the center of the couch, supported both her arms with pillows, and delicately placed Tony in her arms. She hovered nervously next to her, ready at any second to catch Tony, should Rachel drop him.

I held my breath, hoping that Rachel wouldn't protest when the time came to hand Tony back. She didn't. She held him and kissed him, then gently passed him back to Jenny.

That was the last time our family saw baby Tony. We hear, though, that he is thriving in his new family.

We are thrilled to know he is well, but we do think he must miss Rachel, and especially those carefully planned stroller rides.

The LORD bless you, my daughter.

—RUTH 3:10

PART TWO

Family
Ties

CHAPTER NINE

Who Was That Masked Woman?

*M*y husband and I served as foster parents for four years. As I look back on those years, I see foster parenting as a natural extension of the caregiving role I assume when I perform my duties as a nurse.

♥ ♥ ♥

The nursing profession tends to attract those who are already known to be the designated "caregivers" of their families and friends. Most (though certainly not all) nurses are born with warm, caring, somewhat "motherly" personalities. Their choice of nursing as a career is simply an educational extension of their already caregiving natures.

Predictably, it was a nurse who inspired me to consider foster parenting. Yvonne and I worked in the ICU together. She was an extremely compassionate, competent nurse, one who always cared for even the sickest of patients with a great sense of tenderness and dignity.

Though I appreciated her nursing skills, it was Yvonne's long-term position as a foster parent that I admired the most.

She was a great storyteller, and I loved hearing about the antics of the children she and her husband cared for. Some of the little ones placed with them were pleasant, lovable, and funny. Others were understandably distraught and disagreeable.

Yvonne loved them all. She once told me that anticipating a new foster placement felt for her like waiting to open a wrapped Christmas package: She could hardly wait to see what would be inside.

Yvonne and I had been friends for several years when, after months of praying, pondering, and receiving professional training, our family finally became licensed to care for foster children. This new parenting role was imminently rewarding but also truly difficult for our family. During slow times at work I discussed with Yvonne how we were coping with our first placement—an extremely lively and disruptive five-year-old girl. Yvonne listened to me, encouraged me, advised me, and prayed for me.

We cared for four children during the years we served as foster parents. I treasure the memories of those special children, and I will always credit Yvonne with our decision to become a foster family.

Sadly, I know of few happy endings for foster children or for the families who care for them. Generally the children are returned to well-meaning but poorly equipped birth parents, while the foster parents, who have grown to love the children as their own, are left to worry and pray for the children's health and safety. This was by far the most difficult part of our foster parenting experience—the part that haunts me to this day.

Yet *sometimes* the system *does* work.

We were fortunate to experience, with our very last placement, a rare and wonderful storybook ending for one rare and wonderful little boy. Jerome became part of our family when he was eight months old. He came to us not because he had been abused or neglected, but simply because his mother was not physically or emotionally able to care for a child. She loved him very much and she tried extremely hard (with help from Social Services) to gather the strength and abilities she needed to be a good parent. However, due to circumstances beyond her control, it became obvious to her and to everyone involved in her case that even after a year and a half of trying her best, she was still not able to independently parent her son. In a painful, selfless act of love, she released Jerome so he could be adopted. She wanted him to have the life she knew she could never give him.

As soon as Jerome was made available for adoption, his caseworker, Sonia, contacted a childless couple who was seeking to adopt a toddler. Would they be interested in meeting him?

John and Kathy were interested—very interested. In fact, the couple could scarcely bear the two-day wait before their scheduled first meeting with Jerome.

Kathy, wanting to be prepared with a healthy snack should Jerome arrive hungry, bought graham crackers and apple juice.

John, wanting to be prepared should Jerome arrive wanting to play, bought a ball. And a toy telephone. And a miniature car. And a book—just in case Jerome arrived wanting a story.

There was only one major glitch in the planned meeting between Jerome and his prospective new parents.

Grandma.

Though John and Kathy had excitedly phoned everyone they could think of when they learned of Jerome's existence and of their upcoming visit with him, they wanted their first meeting with him to be private. This, they believed, would be an emotional, perhaps overwhelming, situation, and they did not want anyone present except themselves, Jerome, and the caseworker.

Their decision did not sit well with John's mother. It did not sit well *at all.*

"I want to see this baby. I want to hold him. I want to kiss him. If I am going to be this baby's grandma, then I absolutely *should* see him. *Need* to see him. Have a *right* to see him. How could you kids dare tell me not to come? I am *family!*"

But John and Kathy would not be moved. They were sorry. Yes, Grandma would meet Jerome soon—very soon, but not this time. They were not budging. John and Kathy's minds were made up.

The day of Jerome's scheduled first visit was hot and sunny.

Caseworker Sonia drove carefully through John and Kathy's tree-lined neighborhood. Two-and-a-half-year-old Jerome, oblivious to the life-changing nature of this appointment, kicked his feet and chattered noisily beside her.

Sonia eased the car into the driveway, released Jerome from his safety seat, and scooped him up in her arms. Standing in the driveway, she looked around and noted that the street was lined with pretty houses and well-kept lawns. Most of the house's yards were adorned with both blooming flowers and swing sets. Some had basketball goals. The neighborhood appeared to be a good place to raise a child. She was pleased by what she saw.

Sonia knew a neighborhood could not be judged by outward appearances alone—after all, the people living there are what really count. So she was especially impressed by the unusual friendliness of John and Kathy's next-door neighbor. The woman, wearing a huge straw hat and dark, wraparound sunglasses, waved from her perch on a faded pink lawn chair. The chair was positioned in the woman's side yard, the portion of grass directly adjacent to John and Kathy's yard. Not only did the woman wave and wave, but she called out friendly verbal greetings to Sonia and Jerome. Jerome squirmed in Sonia's arms, flashed a moviestar smile in the woman's direction, and waved right back at her.

The visit went well. Jerome ate graham crackers and drank apple juice. He chased the ball, talked on the toy telephone, and made *"vroom-vroom"* noises while pushing the miniature car across the kitchen floor. Finally he fell asleep in John's lap while listening to Kathy read to him from the new storybook.

John and Kathy were in love.

Quickly, way too quickly for his prospective parents, Jerome's two-hour visit was over. Sonia gathered his things. John carried Jerome to the car and Kathy buckled him into his seat.

Sonia looked up and noticed the woman in the straw hat, folding chair in hand, trotting toward her car. It was parked next to the curb in front of her house. Sonia commented to John and Kathy about the friendliness of their next-door neighbor. They glanced at each other quizzically, then looked to the street just in time to see the sunglassed woman's car lurch away from the curb and speed out of sight.

John grinned and shook his head. That woman was no next-door neighbor. They didn't even *have* a next door neighbor, since the house adjacent to theirs had stood vacant for the past three months.

There could be no mistake.

That masked woman was Grandma.

Within a few months, Jerome became John and Kathy's legally adopted son. Friends and family from all across the United States traveled to Texas in order to witness the joyous courtroom finalization of the long process. Afterward, everyone went back to John and Kathy's home for a grand backyard party. Balloons hung from the trees, barbecue scented the air, and baritone-voiced uncles sang and played banjos on the deck.

Stationed right in the middle of the noisy festivities, sitting in a faded pink lawn chair, wearing a big straw hat and dark sunglasses, *and* holding her new grandson, Grandma watched it all. She smiled with great satisfaction.

I wasn't at the party. Neither was my friend Yvonne. In fact, Yvonne and I no longer live in the same town, and I haven't seen her in way too many years. I only heard about the party from John and Kathy.

Even so, I know one thing for sure: If Yvonne and I *had* been at the party we would have worn our big straw hats and our sunglasses. We would have brought our lawn chairs and set them up on either side of Grandma. Yvonne and I would have watched it all and smiled great smiles of satisfaction.

Sometimes there really *are* happy endings.

He settles the barren woman in her home
as a happy mother of children.

—PSALM 113:9

CHAPTER TEN

Waiting for the Irises

Sometimes patients' symptoms just don't relate to a specific diagnosis. They may have pain or discomfort that can't be explained through testing or examination. My job often involves some detective work to determine the cause of such unexplained, worrisome problems. Whether it be headaches, stomach irritation, or shortness of breath, I usually find that my patients hold the origin of these symptoms in their own hearts.

🙼 🙼 🙼

No one would accuse Sally Jeffery of being a frilly woman. She owned five dresses, all belted shirtwaists in shades of blue or gray, all sewn on an ancient treadle machine set up in her back bedroom. She cut her own hair and wore it in a tidy, gray-streaked bun pinned low on her neck. Her home stood plain and devoid of knickknacks, but she dusted every other day. Twice a week she did her laundry, and every Saturday morning she baked her church's communion loaf.

Sally didn't watch television. For entertainment she read paperback Western novels and tended her flowerbeds. Once a month she carted a paper bag with the previous month's books to the Main Street Used Bookstore and traded them for a new supply. The young woman who owned the store saved hard-to-find titles for Sally. In exchange, Sally brought her extravagant, newspaper-wrapped bouquets from her yard.

If Sally was conservative in her approach to fashion and home decor, she let her hedonistic impulses run free in her flowerbeds. Red, pink, and purple petunias spilled beyond the brick borders that had been laid to contain them. Climbing roses crept over and trailed past the board fence enclosing the backyard. Gardenia bushes, heavy with creamy white blossoms, scented the air outside Sally's bedroom window with a fragrance that ensured the sweetest of dreams. In well-prepared beds, giant sunflowers stood in the back, multicolored zinnias and red salvia grew in the middle, and squatty purple violets thrived close to the ground.

Though she appreciated the compliments she received on all her flowerbeds, it was her iris garden that brought Sally annual fame and recognition. She had bought, bartered for, collected, tended, and nurtured irises for 20 years. They were her specialty.

Folks, including entire bus-riding garden clubs, traveled from miles away every year just to see the rare varieties, the amazing sizes, and the unusual colors of the irises that Sally Jeffery grew. Wearing clean cotton work gloves and a new straw hat, she gave personal tours of her garden and answered their questions with a mixture of authority and mystery.

Local and state newspapers featured her on their covers and in their garden sections. A well-worn scrapbook of clippings chronicled Sally's rise to horticultural fame.

Irises have a very short blooming season, and through experience Sally could predict, within a few days, when they would be at their peak. Though generous and humble the rest of the year, when the irises bloomed Sally was so puffed up with pride she was almost dizzy-headed.

Self-multiplying, irises have to be dug up, divided, and thinned every year, but no matter who asked or what price was offered, Sally refused to part with even one prized bulb. Even though she knew some of the covetous garden club ladies called her selfish behind her back, she wouldn't give in.

This year's weather conditions, a dry summer followed by a warm and rainy winter, would, Sally predicted, produce the best irises seen in many years. She was excited about the season, and especially anxious to see the flowers that would sprout from a particular rare bulb she had obtained last fall from a well-guarded, secret supplier.

Just one day before the irises would peak, Sally's son-in-law phoned to tell her that her daughter was in the hospital. Bea had contracted heart-damaging rheumatic fever when she was a child. Though weakness limited her activity and decreased her endurance, she had gone on to teach school, marry, and have a family, but once or twice every year she would develop fluid around her heart and have to be hospitalized for a few days.

Sally carefully weighed her options. Bea's condition didn't sound too serious. It was an eight-hour drive and there was really nothing she could do if she did go. She could wait a week and then go to see Bea and the grandchildren. Once she got there, she could really be of help with the cooking and cleaning. That made much more sense than to go now. Yes, she would definitely wait and go next week.

Just as she predicted, the irises were spectacular that year. Everyone agreed that they had never seen such color, such size, such variety. The garden club ladies were especially impressed by the beauty of Sally's newest variety. Truly, this was one of her best showings ever.

It had been three months since the sudden onset of Mrs. Jeffery's chest pain. Though extensive testing could not find any cause for her angina pectoris, her chest pain, it was truly crippling. As a last resort, she was sent to cardiac rehab, to be treated as if she had experienced an actual heart attack. My assigned task was try to help Sally return to her previous level of functioning.

I taught her diet modification, exercise routines, and relaxation techniques, but Mrs. Jeffery continued to have severe, frightening chest pain every day. She could be sitting in church, at home with the newspaper, or shopping for tomatoes when the crushing pain would hit her. She made repeated trips to the emergency room, where after cardiograms, X-rays, and blood tests she would be sent home, told once again that her heart was fine.

I tried to talk to her, to discover if she was under stress. I asked if something was troubling her or was bothering her, but she only shook her head. The chest pain continued.

Then one day Mrs. Jeffery told me about her beloved irises—about how this had been their most beautiful year ever. She told me how her daughter Bea had become ill, and how she waited until after the irises bloomed to go to her.

She told me her only daughter, Bea, died the day before she arrived. The pain in her heart had been with her ever since.

One night shortly after our conversation, Sally couldn't sleep. She got out of bed and went to her iris garden. She stood looking at the plot for several long minutes. Then, in the moonlight, she knelt in the dirt. Sally began to dig. Faster and faster, first with her bare hands, then with a trowel and later a shovel, she dug. She worked all night, but by daybreak she had dug up every single iris bulb and thrown them in a huge pile. She struck matches, one after another, and threw them onto the pile of bulbs. She stood barefoot in her dirt-stained nightgown and watched the bulbs burn up until nothing was left but the acrid smell of ashes.

Sally never came back to cardiac rehab. She didn't need to. The chest pain stopped as suddenly as it had begun.

The fire left an ugly black scar on the lawn, but on that day, the last day of the irises, the scar on Sally's heart began to heal.

> *Man born of woman*
> *is of few days and full of trouble.*
> *He springs up like a flower and withers away;*
> *like a fleeting shadow, he does not endure.*

> —JOB 14:1,2

CHAPTER ELEVEN

Granny's Gift

Patients in the hospital often receive gifts of flowers or fruit. Sometimes visitors bring along books and magazines or even new slippers or a robe. A special gift a new mother received from her late grandmother is something I will never forget.

❧ ❧ ❧

Marie was a chubby four-year-old when her mother returned to college to finish her teaching degree. Her older brothers were already in school, and Marie would begin kindergarten the next fall. It was decided that Marie would spend the three days a week her mother would be in class at Granny's house.

Though her mother was reluctant to leave her, the arrangement suited Marie and Granny just fine. They had always been close and looked forward to having time alone with each other.

Their mornings together began with jelly sandwiches, despite Marie's mother's insistence that her daughter had already eaten breakfast. Granny would just smile and slather a little more butter and grape jelly onto a slice of Wonder bread, and Marie would smile back and climb right onto a

61

chair stacked with two fat Sears catalogs so she could reach the table.

After breakfast Granny washed the dishes. Marie stood in a chair and helped dry. Granny put the dishes away and Marie placed the silverware in the drawer. Together they swept the kitchen floor. Granny swept with a big broom, and Marie used one with a sawed-off handle that was just her size.

On sunny days, Granny washed clothes and hung them on the line to dry. Marie handed her the clothespins and moved the basket for her. Sometimes Granny and Marie would dust or run the carpet sweeper, and every Monday they changed the sheets on all the beds, even the extra beds that no one slept in.

After morning chores, Granny would be tired, so if the weather was warm, they sat on the porch and just talked. Granny told Marie stories. The ones Marie liked best were about when her daddy was a little boy. She especially loved to hear of times when her daddy was naughty or when he and his brother and sisters got into trouble.

For lunch, Granny cooked macaroni and cheese and barbecued wienies, tuna fish salad sandwiches and Fritos, or chicken noodle soup and crackers. They always ate dessert, usually coconut cake, egg custard pie, or soft cookies that Granny called tea cakes. Marie's favorite was barbecued wienies and custard pie. Granny liked tuna sandwiches and tea cakes best.

Granny believed little girls needed naps every day. After lunch, she made a pallet out of two folded quilts laid down on the living room floor beside her recliner. She turned on the television to watch her "story" and told Marie to go to sleep because she needed to rest. Marie would try. She would close her eyes as tightly as she could for as long as she could, but after just a few minutes, Marie would hear Granny begin to snore, and she would prop herself up on her elbows and watch the end of As the World Turns.

When the weather turned cooler, Granny set up her quilting frame in the living room. Hung from the ceiling, the rectangular quilt took up almost the entire room. Marie played Barbies on the floor under the frame while Granny worked tiny stitches into the padded fabric suspended above her head. Marie also loved to sit in Granny's lap and practice quilting. In and out, up and down, just like Granny showed her, Marie would push the needle through the quilt top, the cotton batting, and the muslin backing. Her stitches were long, crooked, and loopy, but Granny always bragged on what a good job she did. Marie loved knowing that Granny was proud of her.

Marie was now a maternity patient. She was 20 years old and the new mother of a baby boy. Granny, having lived a good long life, had passed away just two days before the birth of Marie's baby. Though thrilled with her first child, Marie felt sad and wished Granny had lived a few more days to see this great-grandson. She would have once again told her granddaughter that she was very proud of her.

I was checking Marie's blood pressure when her mother came into the hospital room carrying a large brown paper-wrapped box. Marie's name was printed in neat letters on the top. I watched as this new mother grasped the package as eagerly as a child would.

"This is a gift from your Granny," her mother told her gently.

Marie looked up quizzically. Her mother explained that Granny had wrapped the package months ago, and told her to be sure that Marie received it should anything happen to her before the baby came.

Marie slowly removed the brown paper, lifted the lid off the box, and turned back the tissue. Inside the box was not a delicate infant dress or even a pastel baby blanket. The box held a heavy, brightly colored patchwork quilt—what to me appeared to be an old quilt.

I watched as Marie lifted the gift from the box, unfolded it, and laid it across the bed. I admired the colors, the design, and the careful workmanship. I lifted a corner for a closer look and noticed a long row of large, crooked, loopy stitches.

Marie noticed them too, and as new mothers are prone to do, began to weep and smile at the same time. She told me about how Granny had kept her when she was little, how patient Granny always was, how she let her help with whatever needed to be done, and how she always made her feel like she could accomplish anything she tried.

The gift of the quilt was a reminder of how Granny had known just how to make a chubby little four-year-old girl feel competent and special. Granny took pride in her expert quilting, but she had never removed the childish stitches Marie had placed there so many years before. She had left them just as they were and had added her own tiny, tidy stitches alongside them.

Though Granny had known she might not be there in person for the birth of this baby, she had made sure Marie would receive, yet again, a message of love and encouragement.

When Marie's new son was discharged from the hospital, he left snuggled in his mother's arms. She had dressed him in a new outfit, and wrapped up in the brightly colored patchwork quilt.

It was a very cold day and his mother wanted to be sure he would be warm—inside and out.

I have been reminded of your sincere faith,
which first lived in your grandmother.

—2 Timothy 1:5

CHAPTER TWELVE

Thanksgiving on the Mountain

*B*eing a nurse has allowed me to travel. I go to areas of the world that are poorly served by the local medical system. Usually I work with missionaries who minister to the soul while I care for the body. Working in foreign countries has been a great education for me. I have learned that situations before my eyes are often not as I first thought them to be.

❧ ❧ ❧

I'll celebrate Thanksgiving Day in Mexico this year, just as I have the past several years. Twice each year I travel with like-spirited companions to provide medical, dental, veterinary, and spiritual care to the poorest of the poor in remote, rural Mexican villages. American churches finance the medicine and supplies, and they pay for food and transportation for the natives who direct our work. We try hard to blend in, to stay behind the scenes in our sometimes-awkward efforts to serve. Yet it is not always possible, for we also provide a measure of novelty, somewhat like a carnival sideshow that draws in shy or suspicious folks to observe and accept what we have come to give.

On my first medical campaign nine years ago, I spent much of the week trying to control my instantly readable "plastic wrap" face. I wanted neither my tears nor my shock and pity to be visible to the dignified, proud people who seemed to watch my every move.

Control was not easy.

Poverty choked my heart as tightly as the desert dust clogged my nostrils. I saw young boys drive bony cows and oxen to the drought-shrunken, stagnant reservoir. Animals stood shoulder deep in the murky pit. The thirsty beasts drank and drank, ignoring the nearby women filling their families' containers in this shared water source. I watched arthritic grandmothers stagger achingly toward home, shoulders burdened with heavy buckets swinging from crude wooden yokes. In my arms I held thin and pale-eyed children—anemic, frail legacies of chronic infestations of intestinal parasites, common in areas with contaminated water.

Every night, after a long-avoided trip to the stinky outhouse and a baby-wipe bath (water being much too scarce to be used for bathing), I lay on my cot and wept, grateful for the refuge of darkness. I was overwhelmed with sorrow and guilt. My only thoughts were of the contrasts between my comfortable, middle-class, white-bread lifestyle north of the border and the living conditions I was experiencing south of that imaginary line that so divided us.

I spent much of that first trip sad, tired, and overwhelmed.

Years have passed, and my experiences in Mexico are now less troubling to me. I've learned a little of the language and become accustomed to the culture, and I am seldom shocked by what I see.

I've come to know people as individuals. Now I know their names, which couple is expecting a child in the spring, and who has died since my last visit. Like any woman would,

I rejoice with the lucky housewife whose husband is finally building her a new cookhouse. I look forward to catching up on my Mexican friends' lives.

My eyes and my heart now see what my friends and I have in common. Carmen and I have pots of scraggly geraniums on our front stoops. Hers are pink. Mine are red. Neither of us is a very gifted gardener.

Juan tinkers with their cranky old Chevy to keep it running. My husband struggles to do the same with our 11-year-old station wagon.

When Marta's daughter is sick, her face wears the worried expression I've seen in my own mirror.

When I'm a guest at Sofia's table, she spreads her prettiest cloth and scrounges to find enough places for everyone to sit. My home is small too, and I've had to bring in folding lawn chairs to seat my guests. We fuss over whether everyone is comfortable, and we've both been known to work some kitchen magic when the 12 guests we expected not only show up, but also bring along their friends!

Though no longer paralyzed by sadness, I never pretend that life is easy in Mexico. My friends' lives are harsh, and poverty makes facing even simple challenges almost unbearable. Their economic situations stand as precarious as do their houses built of clay and straw.

But I have learned that it is only when I see our commonalities, our sameness, that I move from guilt and pity to compassion and hope, manifested by my actions. Only relationships with those who are both poor in the spirit and poor in the flesh teach me that I am the same as those I attempt to serve, whether in a Mexican clinic or in an American hospital.

The pregnant teenager who worries about her swollen feet and the lonely old man who longs for a granddaughter's bedside visit share the same needs and desires as are common to people all over the world. My job is to care for them as I do for my own flesh, to remember that they, and I, are the same: in need of divine healing from our diseases and our poverty.

This Thanksgiving, the food will be carefully prepared and the outdoor table will be spread with a richly embroidered cloth. Layered in long johns and a heavy parka, I'll feast on roasted goat, beans, tortillas, and chilies.

Hundreds of miles north, my extended family will enjoy turkey, cranberry sauce, and pumpkin pie. My dad will pray over the abundant spread, offering thanks to God for all good gifts. Then his prayer will end, as it does every day, with this sentence:

> *"Father, we pray that each day will find us,*
> *in some way, a blessing to our fellowman."*

Shivering in the frosty Sierra Madre mountains of Mexico, my prayer will be the same.

> *They rested and made it a day of*
> *feasting and joy.*
>
> —ESTHER 9:17

CHAPTER THIRTEEN

Women Who Wait

The lives of the patients I care for make a great impression on me. I am genuinely interested in the stories of their lives, and I learn so much even from their tales. Occasionally bits of information I have almost forgotten come flooding back to me, often with a new rush of meaning and understanding. A recent shopping trip seems an unlikely catalyst for such recall, but it triggered important memories of a patient I had all but forgotten.

❧ ❧ ❧

Mrs. Abbey's heart was giving her lots of trouble. She didn't understand her low-salt diet, and she couldn't seem to remember to take her medicine. As a result, she was retaining fluid. This fluid retention caused her to be short of breath and to have a low activity tolerance. Mrs. Abbey's doctor hoped that visits from a home health nurse would bring her into compliance with both her diet and her medication regime.

Assigned to call on Mrs. Abbey, I arrived at her senior-citizen-designated apartment and rang the bell. After waiting for what seemed to be an unusually long while, the heavy door finally opened and I was greeted by a sweet-faced, slightly blue-haired lady. She invited me into her cozy, doily-draped living room and insisted I have a cup of coffee with her before "getting down to business."

Thus began my relationship with Mrs. Abbey. I checked on her a couple of times a week for several months. During my visits she learned about low-salt foods and medication schedules, and I learned interesting details about her life.

Mrs. Abbey had been a widow for more than 20 years. During their marriage, she and her husband had been blessed with one child, a son. He was named Ed, after her father, and he lived about an hour away. Mrs. Abbey greatly anticipated and enjoyed his weekly visits.

My petite patient always seemed in a good mood. The apartment complex she lived in housed mostly elderly women. From prior visits with other residents, I knew the place was a hotbed of geriatric gossip and that many of the folks who lived there constantly engaged their neighbors in fierce feminine feuds. Yet Mrs. Abbey seemed to get along with everyone. She didn't get upset over situations that had her neighbors up in arms, or at least up on their canes and walkers.

"Mrs. Abbey," I asked, "how did you come to have such an easygoing disposition? Have you always been this way? Were you just born with a sunny outlook on life?"

"Why, of course not, child!" she exclaimed. "When I was younger my quick temper and snappy tongue got me into trouble more times than you want to know. Why, I used to fly right off the handle over almost nothing."

"What happened to change you, Mrs. Abbey?"

"I can't say, Honey. The anger just went away and I'm not troubled by it anymore. Even dogs that bark all night and men who smoke stinky cigars don't get under my skin like they used to. I just get up and open or close my window. I suppose if a person lives long enough maybe she just uses up all the anger in her. All I know is that after 92 years of living, there just isn't any mad left in me."

Interesting concept. I wonder, *Just how long does a person have to live to use up all the mad in him?*

When Mrs. Abbey's son was 19, she told me, he went off to serve in the Army. The country was at war at the time, and it nearly broke her heart to see him go. She remembered like it was yesterday how on the day he left she tried to hide her silent tears, and how as she stood over the sink they had fallen softly into the dirty dishwater.

She had experienced the hardest time sleeping the first few nights Ed was gone. One night, long after her husband had begun his gentle nightly snoring, she eased out of bed. Feeling her way through the dark house, she eased down the hall and out the back door. The moon was full and was bright enough to cast luminous shadows of her figure moving to the back gate. Beside the gate grew a massive live oak tree. Ed had played under the tree as a toddler and climbed in it as a child. Mrs. Abbey knelt under the tree to pray, but instead of bowing her head like she usually did, she looked right up at the moon as if she were staring God straight in the face.

If He would watch over Ed, keep him safe, and bring him back home, she would . . . she would . . . well, she would do anything.

Anything.

Mrs. Abbey returned to her grassy moonlit prayer altar over and over during the months Ed was overseas. She never knew exactly what she was promising to do for God, but she was positive she would do her best to keep up her end of the deal if He would grant her only son safety.

One day after being gone nearly two years, Ed just opened the front door and walked right into the house. He was wounded, but would recover. Mrs. Abbey's desperate wait was over. That night, once again waiting until her husband (and this time her beloved son as well) were asleep, she knelt under the oak tree and looked up at the moon. Her prayer that night was a simple one.

Thank You.

Though Mrs. Abbey would continue to be a praying woman all her life, the night her son was returned to her was the last time she knelt under the oak tree.

I like elderly people. Not only am I fond of old *people*, but I also like old *things*. Ancient quilts, old dishes, and aged framed pictures are particular fascinations of mine. One of my favorite ways to spend an hour or a day is exploring a junk store or an antique shop.

Recently I, with my friends Jeanette and Shelia, took a whole day to travel to a nearby town we had heard offered bunches of such stores and shops. We met at my house and got an exhaustingly early start. My companions and I were not disappointed. We found the tiny city of Gladewater, Texas, to be a virtual storehouse of antiques. At least a dozen-and-a-half store fronts on the main street boasted of having just what we had come foraging for.

My friends and I had a great time that day, beginning with a delicious brunch in a cozy combination cafe-bakery. After our meal we hit the streets. Jeanette and Shelia love old stuff as much as I do, and between the three of us we found several interesting treasures. Jeanette bought a rickety wooden plant stand and two pieces of 1940s Boy Scout memorabilia for her soon-to-be Eagle Scout son, Jacob. Shelia scooped up several pretty glass bowls, and I purchased two frayed crocheted pot holders and a tin canister set ornamented with funky faded cherry decals.

By almost five o'clock, our preset departure time, we had tired feet and empty wallets. It was time to go home, but there was just one more store we wanted to check out on our way out of town. We almost passed it up but decided we had time to make this one last stop.

The cute shop was worth our time. Not only did it have good junk, but truly unique craft items were on display as well. We three admired the shop owner's artistry and talked each other into splurging on just a few over-budget purchases.

We had paid for our treasures and were about to take our leave when I spied a framed print I had previously overlooked. Rendered in muted shades of blue and green, I found it to be captivating—somehow even mesmerizing. Jeanette and Shelia agreed the picture was interesting, but didn't really share my unexplainable enthusiasm for it.

The simple scene inside the scarred wood frame was of three human figures. One of the figures was a woman of about 50, and the other was a girl who appeared to be in her twenties. The younger woman held a blanket-wrapped infant in her arms. The three stood silhouetted on a beach, looking out over a vast, moonlit ocean.

I held the picture in shaky hands and turned it over to check the price. In one corner, written in faded ink but by a once-steady hand, were these words:

They also serve who only stand and wait.

I bought the picture. It was priced way too high and the only way I could pay for it was to use my credit card. Once home, I examined my purchase closely and found it wasn't even an art print but simply an illustration, lovingly clipped from a long-forgotten but well-read woman's magazine.

I have never regretted buying the picture. The scene hangs in my bedroom now. When I see it I remember Mrs. Abbey. I am reminded of how she and women like her the world over *served, and continue to serve, by waiting.*

I honor them, and I say a little prayer for them.

> *I say to myself, "The Lord is my portion;*
> *therefore I will wait for him."*

—LAMENTATIONS 3:24

CHAPTER FOURTEEN

Special Days

S ome of my patients I know for only a few hours or a few days. Others become lifelong friends. Often I develop relationships with the families of my patients. Mary and I became friends after I took care of her mother. We remain friends even today.

❧ ❧ ❧

I'm standing in the post office thumbing through a stack of bills, plus yet another low-interest credit card offer, plus a flyer extolling the adventures I would enjoy if only we owned a satellite dish. I almost miss the bright orange-and-green envelope tucked between the Radio Shack catalog and the weekly church bulletin. When I see the handwriting, I smile. It's from Mary.

Today is November fifth, and my birthday is not until January, but the envelope is scrawled with "Happy Birthday!" and embellished with pencil drawings of wrapped packages and a widemouthed me eating birthday cake. I tear open the card and find six red balloons and a tiny gold daisy-shaped pin for my lapel.

Mary hasn't forgotten when my birthday is, nor is the card late. But then, neither is it exactly early. Mary just doesn't pay much attention to what day it is.

Mary's friends and family have grown accustomed to lovely, hand-embossed Christmas cards in March, and deliveries of gold mums proclaiming "Have a great Thanksgiving" in July. On the first day of December, the 34 widows of Mary's church found gingerbread men, wrapped in purple tissue and tied with silver cord, in their mailboxes. Attached to each little brown man was a note instructing the church ladies to "Have a Very Happy New Year."

Mary flies her American flag every Tuesday and keeps a tiny ceramic Santa on the ledge over her kitchen sink year-round. Children on her street are treated to impromptu parties, complete with hats, balloons, and ice cream sundaes whenever Mary spots a rainbow.

Most people marvel at Mary's spontaneity. Some think she's a bit loopy. Others shake their heads and wonder if she'll ever grow up.

When Mary was a little girl she usually acted pretty grown-up. She was two years younger than her brother Robert. He took the role of protector-defender of Mary very seriously. He looked out after her, and because Mary knew he would always rescue her, she sometimes got herself into scrapes that landed them both in trouble with their parents. They argued and fought as siblings do, yet they were fiercely loyal to each other and very rarely tattled.

Although generally the more responsible of the two, Robert had one weakness: He had trouble waiting . . . and saving . . . and planning ahead. If he and Mary both received candy, Mary squirreled hers away in her room, while he ate his up within a half-hour and begged until she shared hers with him.

Mary saved her allowance in her sock drawer, but Robert spent his on comic books and ammunition for his B.B. gun.

When he ran out of money and had no funds for the movies on Saturday, Mary always, though somewhat grudgingly, loaned him part of her allowance.

Mary could keep a secret; Robert couldn't. Mary sat still in church; Robert squirmed. Mary was chosen three weeks in a row to be class monitor in third grade; Robert went his entire elementary career without holding that distinguished office.

Despite their differences, Mary and Robert loved each other fiercely and collaborated on all kinds of plans and schemes. They were doted on and spoiled by both parents, but Daddy often worked out of town and Mother, having a weak heart, was frequently in bed. Aunt Arla looked after them in the afternoons, but she had modern ideas about rearing children, and neighbors clucked daily disapproval at the freedoms the two enjoyed.

When Mary was eight and Robert was ten, they put their heads together to plan the perfect gifts for their mother. They were successful in their secret quest, and Mother's Day was still more than a week away when Mary carefully wrapped their gifts. Robert chose a salt-and-pepper-shaker set that he had laboriously bejeweled with tiny, glued-on seashells. Mary purchased a pearlized plaster plaque edged in deep rose and embossed with flowers and a Scripture text.

Mary gently placed the gifts on the mantel in the living room and told her mother to be sure not to peek. Robert, though, couldn't stand the excitement and nearly wore out his tissue-wrapped package taking it down, feeling of it, and teasing his mother, trying to get her to guess what was inside.

Finally, on the Saturday morning before Mother's Day, Robert could not stand it any longer. He ran to the living room, retrieved his present, and insisted that his mother open it right then. She protested weakly but looked at his beaming face and tore into the gift. She was delighted with the salt and pepper shakers. Robert smugly returned her grateful hug, and Mary stomped to her room in the sort of huff only a little sister could pull off with such impressive aplomb.

When Mary and Robert awoke the following morning, the *real* Mother's Day, as Mary called it, they were surprised to find Aunt Arla cooking their breakfast. The two were told that their mother had become sick during the night and had been taken to the hospital.

They were concerned, but not afraid. Mother had been in the hospital lots of other times, but she always came home in a few days. Robert and Mary chewed their eggs and toast, then dressed, and then Aunt Arla took them to church with her.

Years have passed and Mary is a real grown-up now. She still misses her mother, who died in the hospital on that long-ago Mother's Day. Fresh out of nursing school, I held the hand of Mary's mother when she died. I remember the doctor saying plainly that it was just her time.

Mary has treasured mementos and photos of her mother and several of her favorite books. Having these tangible items gives her comfort.

One of the mementos has an extra-special meaning to Mary. She keeps it in her bedroom, where she sees it every day. Mary's most prized possession in the world is a pearlized plaque, edged in deep rose, embossed with a flowers and a Scripture text. It reads:

> *Do not boast about tomorrow,*
> *for you do not know what a day may bring.*
>
> —PROVERBS 27:1

Mary is all grown up now, and she doesn't live by the calendar.

CHAPTER FIFTEEN

The Lighter

*I*t was only after a particular patient no longer needed my care that I heard from his g.and-daughter Katrina the story of an especially meaningful event in his past.

♪ ♪ ♪

The whole family knew that Katrina's older sister Cheryl was the smart one in the family. After she graduated from high school at age 16, Cheryl was awarded a full scholarship to the university she had most hoped to attend. While there she maintained a 4.0 grade point average, and during her senior year she was wooed by four well-known pharmaceutical companies. After carefully weighing her options, Cheryl chose the employer who offered both the tuition reimbursement and the flexible working hours she would need to pursue first her master's degree and later her doctorate.

Mature, levelheaded, and intellectually very gifted, Cheryl rose quickly through the company's professional ranks. She was awarded an elite position in the cancer research department. Her job was demanding and the pace was grueling, but being both single and childless by choice, she found the long hours not exhausting but invigorating.

It had taken a total of 14 years, but at the premature age of 30 Cheryl had reached her lofty academic goals *and* found fulfillment in work she cared passionately about.

Katrina's younger sister Anna, on the other hand, was *born* a little mother. Everyone said so. From the time she was just a tot, Anna tended and nurtured a large family of baby dolls. She fed, changed, and rocked them with as much concern and commitment as any real parent. Years past the age when most other girls abandon their childhood toys for makeup and fashion magazines, Anna continued, alone and behind her closed bedroom door, to play with and care for her "babies."

Eventually Anna grew up a bit and found that real children were even more fun to play with than dolls. She was so good with kids that while still in junior high school she was drafted to be a permanent Sunday morning substitute in the church nursery. As she became a teenager her services were in great demand, and most Friday nights found her babysitting a houseful of rowdy youngsters.

None of the family was surprised when, at age 19, Anna married her high-school sweetheart and in four years produced four beautiful babies. She took to motherhood like a duck to water and was the most content person in the world as long as she had a baby on each hip. Her family's yard was the one on the block most littered with toys, and her kitchen counter the one most cluttered with sipper cups and graham cracker crumbs.

By age 24 Anna was exactly where she wanted to be, cozy in her homespun nest, adored by her husband, needed and loved by her children.

Now about Katrina.

When the extended family spoke of Katrina, it was while shaking their heads goodnaturedly. They had always loved her more than she knew, but still—what could be said about middle child Katrina?

She was nothing at all like her sisters.

Though she completed high school with little effort, Katrina did not want to go to college. She could think of no particular career she wanted to pursue. She had no desire to settle down and start a family. She liked to read. She loved nature. She longed to travel.

Katrina knew what she wanted. She worked and saved, and during the June following her senior year, neither forbidden nor encouraged by her parents, she packed up her belongings and moved 500 miles north to a community just outside the gates of a beautiful national park. She had no trouble finding work and happily spent her summer cleaning cabins and maintaining the park's picnic areas.

Dozens of seasonal workers were employed at the park and Katrina forged friendships with other free-spirited folks. She and the other workers spent their days off hiking and canoeing, their nights off dancing and partying.

The adventure she had planned to last a summer lasted a year, and a year turned into three. Money was tight and the park job offered no path for advancement, but Katrina was content.

She missed her family but managed to stay in touch, calling her parents once a month and frequently sending funny postcards to her sisters. When Anna's children had birthdays, she smuggled packs of their favorite forbidden grape bubble gum into their birthday cards. She came home to see them all for a week each Christmas and for a few days each spring.

Katrina's parents worried about her, but her unconventional lifestyle was a fairly harmless one. She was careful to avoid both the illegal and the unhealthy—with one notable exception. She foolishly started to smoke her very first summer away. In the beginning she indulged only at parties, as a way to relax and be sociable. By the time she admitted to the danger of her casual tobacco use, she had developed a pack-a-day habit. Katrina was both surprised and embarrassed when no matter what method she tried, she was unable to quit.

No one in Katrina's family smoked, and on her visits home she went to great lengths to hide her habit from all of them, most especially from her beloved elderly grandparents.

Grandma and Pa, as she and her sisters called them, lived in a tiny frame house whose papered walls were lined with old photos of Katrina and her sisters, and new ones of Anna's children. She had spent wonderful childhood hours basking in their indulgent attention, and she made a point to spend an afternoon with them whenever she was in town.

Some things never change. Grandma was still a chatter-box, while Pa was as quiet as he had always been. Whenever Katrina visited them these days, Grandma's conversation contained endless details about Anna's "precious babies" and Cheryl's job "fighting cancer." She queried Katrina only briefly, not with questions about her job or her life up north, but: *Was she ever going to get married? When was she going to move back home?*

Katrina understood: Grandma meant no harm. Babies and cancer were things she knew and was concerned about. Her own life was so far removed from Grandma's that the older woman could not begin to understand it.

A little more than three years had passed since she had left home the very first time, and Katrina was back for a brief visit. After lunch with her grandparents, Pa asked her if she would care to take a little walk with him. Katrina readily accepted.

They stepped slowly out across the pasture where, in healthier years, Pa had fed cattle. Together they crossed through a grove of pecan trees and sat down on the bank of the property's pond where, on good days, Pa still liked to fish.

He was tired from the short walk, so they sat in silence for a few minutes while he caught his breath.

"Katrina, are you doing all right way off up there? All by yourself and all?"

"Yes, Pa. I'm doing just fine."

"Are you happy?"

"Yes, I think I am."

"That's good, Darlin'."

Silence.

"Katrina?"

"Yes, Pa?"

"I know you smoke."

Katrina's face grew hot.

"I've known about you smoking for a long time." Pa reached into his pocket. "I'm getting old, and there's something of mine I want you to have." His voice caught. "But you cain't tell your gran'ma I give it to you. Do you hear?"

"Yes, sir."

Katrina held her breath, and into her outstretched palm Pa reverently placed his ancient Zippo brand cigarette lighter.

"I quit smoking years ago. It ain't good for you and you ought to quit. But maybe you'll want to use this until you do."

Katrina stood up and told this story at Pa's funeral. He had been a home health patient of mine for more than a year. I had grown close to Grandma and Pa, as they insisted I call them, and so I had come to pay my respects.

The story of Pa's gift brought questions to my mind.

What do you say about a grandpa who gives a granddaughter—one who is fighting a smoker's cough—a cigarette lighter? What message does a gift like that convey?

For Katrina, the young woman who was neither driven nor domestic, but was determined to find her own path, the message was plain:

"I know you far better than you think I do. I love you just the way you are."

What do you say about a gift like that?

Katrina knew exactly what to say. "Thank you, Pa."

And they bowed low to pay him honor.

—Genesis 43:28

PART THREE

*In Sickness
and in Health*

CHAPTER SIXTEEN

Tidings of Charlie and Joy

r. Charlie was 98 years old when he was placed in my care. He had lived through one depression, two world wars, and several U.S. presidents. He had many fascinating stories to tell, and I was a very willing listener.

✿ ✿ ✿

On the day of his disappearance, Mr. Charlie got out of bed at dawn and, moving as quietly as he could, dressed in yesterday's khaki pants and a clean plaid shirt. He put on his shoes and tiptoed carefully past Irma Lee's open bedroom door, down the hall, and into the kitchen. Grateful he had made it this far without waking her, Mr. Charlie tucked a loaf of light bread, a jar of mayonnaise, some sweet pickles, and half a package of hot links into a brown paper bag. He didn't take time for breakfast, but indulged in a long drink of buttermilk straight from the carton.

Mr. Charlie was going fishing. TODAY. He had been asking and asking Irma Lee to take him, but her arthritis had been acting up and she just hadn't felt up to making the mile-long hike to the pond. No matter. He didn't need a babysitter. He would rather fish by himself any day.

Daughter Irma Lee was good to him, and he loved her to pieces, but Mr. Charlie never could figure out how that girl got to be so bossy. Oh, she would be mad when she woke up and found him gone, but he supposed she would get over it in time.

Mr. Charlie dug in the freezer looking for bait. The package of chicken livers he found would do just fine. He popped them into his lunch bag. With his walking stick in one hand and his cane pole and the bulging paper bag in the other, Mr. Charlie set out limping toward one of the best fishing holes in three counties.

Irma Lee was terribly frightened when she woke up that morning and found her daddy gone. She immediately called the neighbors, the sheriff, and the Methodist preacher. Everyone set out hunting for Mr. Charlie. They looked day and night, but by the third day of his disappearance, the tired, sad-faced search party all but gave up on finding the old man alive.

It was four days after Mr. Charlie's disappearance when a woman whose home was a good three miles from Irma Lee's house looked up from washing her breakfast dishes. From her kitchen window she was shocked to see a half-naked old man laid out under her backyard clothesline. She was sure he was dead but called for an ambulance anyway.

Barefoot, muddy, and wearing only his pants, Mr. Charlie was brought by paramedics to the hospital for examination and treatment. After being lost in the woods (and at some point likely submerged in a pond), he was dehydrated and covered with insect bites, cuts, and scratches. Even so, it was amazing to everyone that Mr. Charlie had suffered no serious injuries and was not acutely ill. The doctor who examined him told Irma Lee she would probably be able to take him home in a few days.

Mr. Charlie was admitted to my unit, and once he was settled into a hospital bed I began to clean him up. He was exhausted and slept through most everything I did. Mr. Charlie's daughter, Irma Lee, stayed in the room. She helped me as I bathed him, shampooed his hair, and positioned him comfortably in bed. I commented on the obvious love and devotion she had for her dad.

As we worked, Irma Lee told me about her daddy's life.

When he was just 15 years old, he fell in love with a beautiful 20-year-old woman named Joy. The two were crazy about each other, but the difference in their ages created quite a community scandal. Tongue-wagging only increased when just two months after their courtship had commenced, the pair announced their intent to marry each other. Joy was a little embarrassed, but Mr. Charlie didn't care one bit. He loved Joy so much he would have fought a bear for her.

On their planned wedding day, the two set out walking hand in hand. It was seven miles to town but it didn't even seem like a mile to the young lovers. Mr. Charlie was so thrilled to be getting married that he jumped and skipped and even turned a few cartwheels on the way. This was the best day of his life.

Sadly, his happiness didn't last the whole day. At the courthouse, the eager groom was stunned when he was told by a sour-faced clerk that he was too young to get married without his daddy's permission. There were *no* exceptions.

Mr. Charlie was so upset he cried all the way home.

The next day, unable to bear the misery of his lovesick son, Mr. Charlie's daddy took a whole day off his job and went with the couple back to the courthouse. He signed the necessary papers and the two were married that very afternoon.

Mr. Charlie and Joy *stayed* crazy about each other and enjoyed 61 years together. Early in the marriage they were blessed with six healthy children, but times were hard and they had little in the way of material goods. Joy kept chickens and a garden, and Mr. Charlie worked long hours at any backbreaking job he could get. It took a lot of doing to support such a large family.

"I don't know how my daddy managed it," Irma Lee told me, "but he gave us a good home. I don't remember ever going hungry."

It was about a year before Mr. Charlie's fishing expedition that Irma Lee first noticed that her daddy's mind was beginning to wander. Mr. Charlie remained pleasant enough, but he was forgetful and often confused about where he was. He didn't eat right and she learned he had fallen, several times, in his own backyard. It became obvious to Irma Lee that it was no longer safe for her daddy to live alone. Somewhat reluctantly, but fairly obediently, Mr. Charlie sold the homestead and moved in with his daughter.

We finished his bath and Mr. Charlie began to snore loudly. At my urging, Irma Lee went home to catch a nap and change her clothes. I promised her I would call if I noticed any changes in her daddy's condition.

She hadn't been gone ten minutes when Mr. Charlie woke up. *Resurrected* might be a better way to describe what he did. Rousing from the deepest of sleep, he was suddenly alert and sitting up in bed, hungry and talking up a storm.

I brought him a sandwich, fruit, and a cup of ice cream. He gobbled up the meal, wiped his mouth, took a deep breath, and began to talk.

"Pleased to meet you, nurse. My name's Charlie. Let me tell you a little bit about myself. I'm staying with my daughter for now but I did a lot of traveling in my younger days. I traveled with Dr. King. Yes, girl, I was with Dr. Martin Luther King when he first started giving speeches. We were good friends."

I was surprised and impressed. Irma Lee hadn't mentioned this part of her daddy's life.

"I saw history in the making, I did." Mr. Charlie spoke with great pride and dignity. "I stood behind Dr. King when he spoke and beside him when he marched."

I couldn't believe I was listening to someone who had actually witnessed such historical events. How honored and humbled I was to meet this man and to hear such incredible memories.

"Once Dr. King was giving a speech outside, right beside a river. All of a sudden I heard someone shouting for help. The women started yelling and crying and I saw someone was drowning in that river. I jumped right in the water, swam to the middle, and pulled that man out." Mr. Charlie told me the story with relish and intense satisfaction.

"Turns out the man in the water was somebody I already knew."

"Really? Who was it, Mr. Charlie?"

"Abraham Lincoln. He was my friend too."

When Irma Lee returned I told her about Mr. Charlie's story. She chuckled and wasn't a bit surprised. In his old age he had begun telling tall tales, always involving famous people and amazing feats of courage and strength. He liked to impress people, to watch their reactions.

None of the stories were true.

I smiled, but I admit I was a bit disappointed. I had hoped that at least *some* parts of the yarn had a basis in reality.

I cared for Mr. Charlie during the rest his hospital stay and I heard quite a few more tall tales. I enjoyed both him and his stories immensely.

As I spent time with Mr. Charlie and his devoted daughter, I realized I was actually pretty impressed with the *true* story of his past. There had been some *real* acts of courage in his life, and I wanted to hear more about them. One morning I drew a chair close to his side and sat down.

"Mr. Charlie," I began, "did you ever know a girl named Joy?"

His eyes began to twinkle, he took a deep breath, and then he began to talk.

Weeping may endure for a night,
but joy cometh in the morning.

—PSALM 30:5 KJV

CHAPTER SEVENTEEN

The Anniversary

My position as a nurse has given me a window in which to peer into my patients' lives at some of their most vulnerable moments. I have witnessed situations so intimate and private that I wished myself invisible. I tried very hard to allow Sam and Lily their privacy at just such a moment.

❧ ❧ ❧

They had been playmates and sweethearts since they were barefoot seven-year-olds playing in the dirt together. They had married, amid the dire warnings of their families and the secret envy of their friends, at age 17. They had, they liked to say, "practically raised each other."

Full of all the bravado that a married man not yet old enough to vote could muster, Sam had checked them into the Aloha Best Western Motor Inn. Their chosen honeymoon destination was not Hawaii, as one might assume, but San Antonio, Texas. A ragged palm tree planted under the sign and a seascape hung in the lobby lent an aura of authenticity to the motel's island motif.

Once in the motel room, the powerful teenage desire, which had relentlessly challenged Lily's resolve to be a virgin bride, seemed to vanish. She had purchased—at Sears—the most beautiful nightgown she ever laid eyes on. Fashioned of white tulle, the bodice was trimmed with yards and yards of nylon lace. The gown had hung on the closet door in her girl-hood room, and she had dreamed for weeks of this night, when she would wear it for Sam.

Now, stalling in a bubble bath, with her new husband waiting just outside the locked door, the gown looked not inviting and pretty, but scary, and much more adult than Lily felt. Filled with the terror of the child she was, Lily began to cry. She ran more water in the tub so Sam wouldn't hear.

After what seemed like hours to Sam, Lily gathered up every ounce of courage in her pubescent body. She slipped on the gown, sprayed a cloud of cologne, wiped her eyes, and opened the bathroom door.

It took a moment for Lily's eyes to adjust to the dimness in the bedroom.

Then she saw him. Looking nervous, unsure, and eager, Sam was waiting in the king-sized bed. He gave her what he hoped was a "Come here, woman" look, threw back the cov-ers, and patted the mattress beside him.

The move didn't quite produce the response he had had in mind. When Lily saw his carefully chosen attire, her ner-vous fear dissolved. She began to giggle.

Sam looked at Lily, then at his pajamas. He had bought them—black, with enormous, glow-in-the-dark red hearts—because he thought they were perfect for what he was sure would be the most perfect night of his life. For an instant, Sam was stunned by Lily's reaction. Then he joined her in what was the beginning of a marriage filled with laughter.

So Sam and Lily grew up together. Often Sam told audi-ences that if he had known how much fun married life would be, he would have married Lily when they were 14. Lily bragged that in all these years of life together, she had never filled the car's gas tank and Sam had never filled his iced-tea glass.

Their marriage not only brought joy to each other, but also to the large family they raised. Neighbors chuckled about how, after all these years, Sam and Lily could still be found cuddling in the front porch swing on warm summer evenings.

Sam and Lily's intimacies began with laughter, but they were to end with tears. It was not a party that brought me to Sam and Lily's home on their anniversary.

No candles, flowers, gifts, or fancy foods were in sight. The ugly tools of my trade filled their chintz-decorated bedroom. An oxygen machine hummed next to the bed. Boxes of sterile dressings, adhesives, cleansing solutions, soothing ointments, and colostomy bags threatened to overflow the antique oak table that had been moved into the room to serve as a work service. As a home health nurse, I had become a necessary though reluctantly invited guest in this home.

At first I was confident that Lily could become competent at caring for her colostomy. Having little experience in this specialized type of care, I had read everything I could find and spent hours on the phone with nurses who were experts at caring for new colostomy patients.

However, Lily was depressed, often nauseated, and so weakened by her aggressive cancer that it soon became obvious she never would be able to care for her colostomy.

Sam always excused himself from the room when I cared for the colostomy. When I told Lily I wanted to teach him how to provide her care, I realized she hadn't yet let him see the quarter-sized opening on her abdomen. After many tears and with much convincing from Sam and me, Lily reluctantly let Sam look.

Sam showed no resistance or squeamishness about caring for the colostomy. I used a felt-tipped marker to draw a colostomy stoma on my inner arm and he practiced cleaning it, examining it, and applying a bag just as he would on the real one.

The day had come, on this their anniversary, for Sam to clean and care for Lily for the first time. She was as reluctant to participate in this physical intimacy as she had been 30 years before. Sam was as gentle and persistent as he had been with his reluctant bride.

So rapt was his concentration. So steady were his hands. So soft was the tear that slid down Lily's face.

I stood, quietly, in the silent corner of their bedroom, available if they needed me but unable to raise my eyes. My very presence felt awkward and intrusive in this sanctuary of their marriage. Not in a steamy romance novel or a racy Hollywood film would I have been privy to such intimacy and passion. Some moments between a husband and a wife were never meant to be seen by a stranger's eyes.

Do not cast me away when I am old;
do not forsake me when my strength is gone.

—PSALM 71:9

CHAPTER EIGHTEEN

Sleeping Double

In my work as a home health nurse, I have come across many complex problems requiring creative solutions. Sometimes my ideas work perfectly and the problem is solved. Unfortunately, there are other times when I miss the mark completely. Such was the case with Mr. and Mrs. Johnson.

❧ ❧ ❧

I could not determine what was causing Mrs. Johnson's feet to swell. True, she had a diagnoses of congestive heart failure, making her feet prone to swelling, but for several months (since we had gotten her medication regulated) they had been normal. She was taking a diuretic, a potassium supplement, and digitalis to strengthen and regulate her heart.

We nurses were setting up her medicine in a pillbox with a compartment for each dose. Mrs. Johnson also had Alzheimer's disease and couldn't be counted on to remember to take her medicine, so the home health aides who visited twice a day reminded her to take it.

Her lungs were clear and her heart rate was regular. Her blood pressure was normal and she was not short of breath. The swelling just didn't make sense.

I asked her husband, Tom, about her diet. Some patients are very sensitive to salt, and even a small increase in their sodium intake can cause problems, usually swelling or high blood pressure. He assured me that his wife's meals had not changed. She had not eaten anything out of the ordinary.

It was Lana and Tina, home health aides, who finally discovered the problem. Lana went every morning to Mrs. Johnson's house to bathe her and to help her get dressed for the day. Mrs. Johnson loved to wear brightly colored beads and lipstick, and insisted on wearing a full slip every day. No matter how many folks Lana had yet to see, she was always patient and tender in her care of Mrs. Johnson.

In the evening, Tina helped Mrs. Johnson get ready for bed. She would give her a partial bath, rub her back with rose-scented lotion, and dress her in a soft nightgown.

Mrs. Johnson had always gotten up before Lana's arrival in the morning, but as her Alzheimer's disease progressed, she began to sleep later. Lana discovered, by arriving before Mrs. Johnson got up, that she was sleeping with her feet hanging off the bed. Her feet weren't just a bit off the bed, but hanging down from the knees. This peculiar sleeping position explained the swelling.

There was an easy solution to the problem: I would contact the local medical supply rental company and have a hospital bed with rails delivered and set up at the Johnson home.

Mr. Johnson was a thoughtful man, a man of few words. He was kind to his confused wife but didn't exactly know what to do with her either. We nurses tried not to be bossy with him, but generally he went along with anything we suggested regarding his wife's needs. If we told him she needed a special lotion or some new nightgowns, he was quick to purchase them for her, but he seemed to prefer to stay in the background and let us direct his wife's care.

Mr. Johnson was not one to share his worries and concerns. I do know that his life was not easy. He did the cooking and the laundry, as well as what little cleaning was done. Their children lived out of state, and he was not able to leave Mrs. Johnson for a minute for fear she would wander off.

I always supposed that he loved his wife, but I saw her as more of a difficult, occasionally unruly child than as his beloved companion. I felt sorry for him, though he never voiced a complaint.

Mr. Johnson listened attentively when I told him about the bed. It would have rails that could be raised and lowered, with a plastic-covered mattress, and the head and foot could be positioned up or down. I explained that it would be more convenient for them both. He politely agreed and we moved the double bed in their bedroom over against the wall. The room was large enough for both beds and they could sleep in the same room.

The hospital bed was delivered the very next day. Tina made it up with flowered sheets, a pretty quilt, and ruffled throw pillows. Mr. Johnson agreed that it was a nice bed.

It was just as I had thought. Within a week of getting Mrs. Johnson into the railed bed, the swelling in her feet went down. I was proud of how we had discovered the problem and found a workable solution. Evidently the bed was so comfortable that Mrs. Johnson was getting a better night's sleep. Since getting the new bed, she was up and sitting at the kitchen table with her morning coffee and toast when Lana arrived to bathe and dress her.

One chilly fall morning, a month or two after getting the bed for the Johnsons, I arrived a bit earlier than usual. It was time to test Mrs. Johnson's blood, and I needed to take the sample before she ate her breakfast.

Mr. Johnson answered my knock and seemed a bit unsettled at my unexpected early arrival. Mrs. Johnson was still in bed. I told him that there was no problem. I needed to take a blood sample and it would be even easier for me to perform the venipuncture while she was lying down. I went on back to the bedroom.

I was startled to find the hospital bed neatly made up, but empty. Mrs. Johnson was across the room, contentedly snoring in their double bed. The sheets, blankets, and quilt had been carefully tucked in tightly around her feet.

Mr. Johnson explained to me that the weather had become cooler, and since they only had one electric blanket, he had begun putting her to bed with him. That way they could share the blanket and neither of them would get cold.

I immediately expressed my concern about electrical safety. Mrs. Johnson was incontinent. She wore adult diapers, but her bed was always soaked by morning. The combination of a wet bed and an electric blanket was a dangerous one.

"*Well, Miz Smith,*" Mr. Johnson told me shyly, "*there's not too much danger. You see, I don't exactly plug that blanket in.*"

I learned something in that gentle moment. In my hurried attempts to "fix" problems, I sometimes overlook what my patients and their families need most of all. Like Mr. and Mrs. Johnson, most of us need love and companionship more than we need anything else.

Since then, I have tried very hard to slow down and really listen. Most often, the answers I seek are found not in a piece of expensive medical equipment but in my patients' hearts.

We sent that bed right back to where it came from. I explained to the owner of the rental company that I had made a mistake. Mrs. Johnson didn't need a new bed after all. Her old bed was just fine.

Many waters cannot quench love;
rivers cannot wash it away.

—SONG OF SONGS 8:7

CHAPTER NINETEEN

Gertie and Jeb and the Marriage Bed

ollowing surgery, Gertie needed me to help manage her abdominal dressing. However, she was normally a very independent woman. For more years than I have lived, she and her husband handled a troubling health problem without any outside medical help.

❧ ❧ ❧

Gertie and Jeb enjoyed a thoroughly modern marriage years before it became fashionable to do so. Gertie had always loved her job at the bank, so even after they married, she kept on working. This suited Jeb just fine. He wanted Gertie to be happy, and he saw no reason she should quit her job. He learned to overlook the preacher's pointed Sunday morning comments about men who didn't provide for their families, and together they ignored Gertie's older brothers' frequent jabs about "working wives" who didn't stay home and take care of their families.

It is said that smells can trigger strong memories. Perhaps it was the potent aroma of the "green alcohol" I gently rubbed on Gertie's legs that prompted her to remember an event that happened in the seventeenth year of her marriage.

Like most of my elderly, homebound patients, Gertie believed that a bath in old-fashioned, emerald-colored, menthol-infused rubbing alcohol would cure just about any ailment a person might have. She was *sure* it helped loosen up the stiffness in her arthritic joints. Though I've never been completely convinced of the smelly stuff's medicinal benefits, once I finished changing her postoperative abdominal dressing, I was happy to indulge her with a green alcohol rubdown.

I had successfully nursed Gertie through major surgery, and she was almost completely recovered. Though I believe she *liked* me, Gertie was never able to hide the disapproval she felt at my dismal fashion sense. My work wardrobe, the only garments she ever saw me wear, consisted of brightly colored, pajama-like scrub suits, matching cotton socks, and high-top leather athletic shoes. These casual on-the-job outfits were both practical and comfortable, and, I also like to think, neat and attractive.

Gertie did not agree.

She took great pride in her appearance, and though she rarely left home, Gertie believed strongly in the great importance of "keeping oneself up." Every day she wore a full slip and stockings under a cute cotton housedress. She owned an extensive collection of floral print house slippers, and she always wore a carefully coordinated pair.

Gertie had planned to stop working once she had a child, but after 15 years of being Jeb's wife, she was still mother to no one. As sometimes happens in a childless marriage, she and Jeb became extremely close. The bond they shared didn't begin to make up for their disappointment at not becoming parents, but as the years passed they found themselves treating each other more and more tenderly. It was as if all the attention they had stored up to lavish on a child *had* to be squandered somewhere, so they spent it on each other.

The unusual way the couple got along did not go unnoticed by their peers. Jeb took a lot of teasing about being henpecked, and Gertie's coworkers cattily commented on how Gertie coddled Jeb. Jeb and Gertie didn't pay them any mind. They just good-naturedly shrugged off their friends' jealous comments and went right on spoiling each other.

Gertie, like the other female bank employees, took great care with her personal appearance. None of the bank ladies would have dreamed of leaving their houses without powdering their noses and painting their lips, nor would they have dared dress for work without first putting on layers of rigid instruments of womanly torture (innocently called "foundation garments"). It was also just assumed that any truly stylish working woman would wear sheer stockings and dainty high heeled shoes every day.

Devotion to fashion has its cost, and three-inch heels extort an especially high price. Gertie's consistent choice of elevated footwear made her legs and feet hurt. When she would arrive home from work in the evening, she would kick off her shoes and stockings the minute she got inside the door. Relieved to be out of the torturous high heels, Gertie would pad barefoot around the kitchen whistling and singing as she cooked Jeb's supper.

Most evenings, after they finished washing and drying the dishes, Jeb would take Gertie by the hand and lead her to his great-grandmother's padded rocker. Once she was seated, he would kneel down in front of the chair, take her tired feet in his hands, and give them a gentle massage.

Gertie would close her eyes, sigh, and think to herself that heaven couldn't be a much better place than her own living room.

Most nights after Jeb's delicious foot rub, Gertie would be so relaxed that she would go right to bed, fall sleep, and doze undisturbed all night. Sometimes, though, especially after standing all day, she would be awakened by terrible leg cramps. She and Jeb would be sleeping, cozily spooned side by side, when one of her calves would tighten up. Blissfully unconscious, Jeb would suddenly be jolted awake by his wife's cries of pain.

The first time it happened they had been married for only two weeks. Jeb was wakened from a deep sleep by the awful sound of his new bride moaning and flailing beside him. That first experience just about scared him to death, and at the time he didn't have a clue about what to do to help her. However, after years of marriage he had perfected a well-rehearsed routine for quickly relieving her agony.

The system worked like this: Gertie would yelp, then Jeb would sit up, bolt from their bed, and sprint down the hall to the bathroom. He would fetch the bottle of green alcohol, race back to the bed, and rub Gertie's leg until the cramp was relieved.

After years of practice, Jeb could perform these nocturnal ministrations with the efficiency of an experienced fireman putting out a minor grass fire. He could be out of bed, down the hall, and back into bed before his side of the sheets could even get cold. Eventually Jeb didn't even have to be fully awake to get the job done, and some mornings the only reminder he had of his interrupted sleep would be the lingering aroma of menthol on his hands.

One night, in their seventeenth year of wedded bliss, Gertie woke once again with one of her cramps. This was an especially bad one, and she couldn't even move. Jeb dutifully trotted down the hall to the bathroom, grabbed the familiar bottle, stumbled back to Gertie, and began vigorously rubbing her legs with the smelly solution.

After being married for this long, Jeb had given Gertie maybe a hundred rubdowns. This time, though, something was different.

Predictably, within seconds, Gertie's leg cramp was relieved and Jeb was back in bed beside her. But something was wrong. Her leg—it felt slippery and strange. Just as Jeb began to snore, Gertie reached up to turn on the bedside lamp.

To her horror, her left leg was covered with a thick, frothy white substance. Absent were the characteristic fumes of her beloved green alcohol. Jeb raised up beside her and rubbed his eyes. They began to burn.

"*What* did you put on my leg?"

"Why, green alcohol, of course."

"I don't *think* so!"

Turns out Jeb had picked up the shampoo bottle by mistake. It was the same size and shape as the alcohol bottle and had been sitting right next to it in the medicine cabinet. Jeb's liberal application of the shampoo and his two-handed massage of Gertie's leg had worked it up into a thick foamy lather.

After Gertie's initial shock subsided and Jeb's sleepy head cleared, they got tickled. Gertie playfully accused him of shampooing her leg on purpose, and Jeb insinuated she had switched the bottles' positions in the medicine cabinet just to see if he was paying attention.

Gertie got up and rinsed off her freshly shampooed leg, and Jeb got out of bed and made them both a cup of hot cocoa. It was almost time to get up anyway.

I asked Gertie to tell me the secrets I needed to know to enjoy a happy, modern marriage like she and Jeb had. She told me young folks nowadays make everything way too hard. Aside from me working on improving my wardrobe, she told me all my husband and I needed to do was remember the four Ls:

The four Ls?

Yes.

Love freely.

Lavish each other with attention.

Laugh when things don't go as planned.
And most important, *label all bottles.*

> *Marriage should be honored by all,*
> *and the marriage bed kept pure.*
>
> —HEBREWS 13:4

CHAPTER TWENTY

Dreams of the Old

A poster hanging in my husband Randy's office reads, *"If you can dream it you can achieve it."* He uses this phrase to motivate his students to study longer, his athletes to train harder. Randy believes dreams help determine our destinies. I'm of the opinion that dreams, circumstances, hard work, and grace *all* combine to determine what we can achieve.

L♥ L♥ L♥

When I was a little girl, I lay in my bed and dreamed the simplest of dreams. What I wanted more than anything in the world was to grow up, marry a handsome man, have two children, and live in a little house of my own.

I wanted the very same things when I got older and started high school. So did my best friends, Tanye, Lisa, and Sharon. We spent more hours naming our future children than we did discussing our spring prom dresses. We planned kitchens with checked curtains in the windows, and our graduation gifts to each other were tea towels, coffee mugs, and mixing bowls.

Sometime during my teens I also began to dream of a career as a registered nurse. Encouraged by a favorite teacher,

I applied to nursing school and was accepted. Only a few days after my high school commencement, I began preparing myself to follow in the footprints of Florence Nightingale's polished white shoes.

Those years spent in nursing school were grueling, but the same week I finished I married the dark-haired husband of my desire. Red-checked curtains hung in our tidy little house, and I drank my morning coffee out of a graduation mug. Before celebrating our second wedding anniversary, a son was born to us. Three years later we had a daughter.

All my girlhood dreams had come true.

Who can say what shaped my childhood desires? If I had spent hours gazing at the heavens, perhaps I would have become an astronaut. Professional golf might have been my avocation had my family been country club members. As it turns out, my dreams, daringly domestic for a girl growing up in a liberated woman's world, have brought me great happiness and satisfaction.

The relationship between the dreams and desires of my childhood and the realities of my grown-up life is a mystery to me, but I know for as long as I can remember that my dreams have also been my prayers.

Some circumstances, when remembered, seem more like distant stories than reality. At one such moment in my life, I felt as if I were a make-believe character living out a fairy-tale fantasy.

Never as a child or as an adult had I dared even imagine the reality that stretched below me. From my seat on the plane I could view a land I would never have guessed my eyes would see. Asked to participate in this special medical mission campaign, I was embarking on a once-in-a-lifetime trip to Africa.

For two weeks I was to work beside famous doctors, talented nurses, and dedicated missionaries in the African country of Ivory Coast. Many of the team members were professionals I had previously heard speak and had often read about in missionary journals. For me to have the chance to work beside such legends of faith and service was a thrill I cannot describe. The thought that I would ever visit Africa was as far beyond my wildest expectations as traveling to Mars would have been for a more adventurous soul.

My teammates and I set up mobile clinics in two small villages. We treated patients who had rarely seen a white face and met people who had *never* heard the name of Jesus. While we administered relief for sick bodies, Bible teachers offered relief for sick souls.

Patients came to us with colds, backaches, and weakness, as well as malaria, typhoid, and leprosy. We were able to help some of the people with medications and simple treatments, but others needed more extensive care than we were able to offer.

As is true in any culture, some folks were open and friendly, others shy and reticent. I especially enjoyed watching and listening to the older men and women who came to the clinic. Few people of Ivory Coast live past their mid-fifties, so it was somewhat unusual for us to see a truly elderly patient.

One dignified, ancient-looking man caught my eye. Though he appeared to be about 80 years old, I would guess he was probably only 65. Day after day he came to the clinic site. He would hobble around watching, gesturing, and commenting in his native language almost as if he were there to supervise our whole operation. Though frail, hard of hearing, and unable to walk without his hand-carved cane, the gentleman was obviously a respected community patriarch and a noted village leader. His neighbors nodded politely and interrupted their gossip to speak to him as they mingled with each other and waited for their turns to see the doctors.

Only on the last day of our two-week stay did the old man ask for a medical examination for himself. He was directed to a clinic cubicle and spent an unusually long time in consultation before exiting the room and shaking each of our hands.

I asked the doctor who had seen him what the gentleman's complaint had been. Malaria? Arthritis? Headaches?

No. Not any of those. I learned he had not fathered a child in two years. This problem was *very distressing*. Could anything be done? Was there anything the doctor could give him to help?

We stood in the clinic doorway and watched the old man hike back to the hut he shared with his wife. The sun was beginning to set behind him, and his sandaled feet stirred up a small trail of dust as he walked. I was sure I detected a spring in his limping step.

The smiling young missionary doctor, wisely acknowledging that dreams belong to the old as well as to the young, had given the man a year's supply of vitamins, a prayer, and his very best wishes.

> *Your sons and daughters will prophesy,*
> *your old men will dream dreams,*
> *your young men will see visions.*

> —JOEL 2:28

PART FOUR

Closer Than a Brother

CHAPTER TWENTY-ONE

Nurse Nola

I am indebted to the many older, more experienced nurses I have worked with through the years. My education began when I was in college, but it continues today, as I learn something every day from these seasoned professionals. One of my medical mentors is Nola. She sets an incredible example I strive to imitate.

ℒ♥ ℒ♥ ℒ♥

If I were planning a picnic, I would want Nola on the food committee. If I were organizing a strike, I would want Nola to negotiate. If I were lost, I would give Nola the map.

Nola just *has a way* about her.

We work together at the hospital. I am an RN. Nola is an LVN. In some states her title would be LPN. Because of the differences in our educational backgrounds, I make more money than Nola does. I also have more authority than she does. It is assumed that I will guide Nola, supervise her, and see that she takes good care of her patients.

The truth . . . well, the truth is that Nola has *forgotten* more nursing skills than I have *learned*. She can sneak medicine down a disagreeable toddler so easily he never realizes he's swallowed. She can detect subtle changes in a patient's condition quickly and knows exactly what to do about those changes. Her IV skills are legendary and she knows her medications.

When the doctor on call can't be found, Nola knows where he's "hiding." When an obscure, used-once-every-five-years piece of medical equipment is needed "stat," Nola remembers where, in the vast supply room, it's kept. Nola calms distraught family members and motivates lazy orderlies.

Nola is the person you most want on your team.

In nursing school, students are taught to provide the same compassionate, nonjudgmental attention to every patient placed in their care, regardless of race, color, or creed. I might also add to that instruction: regardless of particular *crime*. Our hospital is located near a prison, and often inmates are brought to us for treatment. Two uniformed armed guards are stationed outside the room, and the prisoners, no matter how sick they are, wear iron shackles on both their arms and their legs. I do my best to provide professional care to these men, trying to treat them as I would any other patient. For me, I confess, this is not an easy task. I am nervous when caring for them, and I struggle to be nonjudgmental. It is impossible for me to completely forget where these men came from and to where they will return.

Juan was a 22-year-old inmate, imprisoned because of murder, hospitalized because of a badly broken arm. I assigned Nola to care for him.

When she made her first morning rounds, Nola found Juan to be quiet and cooperative but in a great deal of pain. He had had reparative surgery the day before. Nola greeted him, checked his vital signs, and changed his dressing. Observing his discomfort, she was quick to give him a pain shot.

Within an hour, breakfast trays arrived on the unit and Nola's patients were served their morning meals. When she noticed Juan's tray was missing salt and pepper packets, Nola brought him replacements from her private stash. She stood and watched him quickly drain his coffee cup. Moments later she brought him a coveted second cup.

After breakfast, Juan, who spoke broken English, asked if he could have a bath. Nola prepared a pan of hot water and laid out a towel and washcloth. She helped him with part of the task, then, ignoring the guards' glances of disapproval, discreetly pulled the room curtain to give him privacy. She also rubbed his feet with lotion and provided him with a toothbrush, a tube of toothpaste, and a small bottle of mouthwash.

After Juan's morning care was completed, Nola changed his sheets, positioned his arm on a soft pillow, and brought him an extra blanket. Before leaving his room, she turned on the television and searched until she located a lively Spanish station. Juan smiled a grateful smile.

The guards, both of whom enjoyed listening to sports on the hospital TV, were a bit less grateful.

Later that morning Juan's surgeon made rounds, applied a cast to the injured arm, and announced that Juan could return to the prison infirmary. The guards notified their superiors, and arrangements were made for his transport.

The prison van had already arrived and was waiting when Nola realized Juan did not have a sling for his arm. While not absolutely necessary, a sling would provide extra support and comfort for the heavy, casted arm. The prison driver and the two guards were understandably anxious to be on their way. But Nola didn't seem to notice. She left them standing in the hall tapping their toes and glancing at their watches while she went in search of a sling. It took her a few minutes to locate the specific type she thought Juan needed and even a few more minutes to adjust it to fit him properly. Finally it was done to her satisfaction and she gave the guards the okay to leave.

As he eased from the bed—shackled, clumsy, and sore— Juan raised his head and looked straight into Nola's eyes.

"Ma'am, I don't know why you treated me so kindly, but I thank you. You took care of me as if I was your own son. I'll never forget you."

Never one to lack just the right words, Nola answered him, "You're welcome, Juan. But from now on, I want you to straighten up your life and behave like a *good* son."

I would like to believe he did.

Go now and leave your life of sin.

—JOHN 8:11

CHAPTER TWENTY-TWO

Growing Up
Is Hard to Do

When we first moved back to the town I grew up in, I ran into old friends and acquaintances almost every day. I would bump into them in the grocery store or end up sitting by them at PTA meetings. Sometimes I would arrive at my hospital nursing job and find myself caring for a long-forgotten school pal or a former teacher. One morning I found myself caring for the father of a former classmate.

⚘ ⚘ ⚘

I knew Joel from high school. He sat beside me in biology class and across from me in world history. We saw each other every day, but we weren't really friends. He was a "cowboy" and I was a "band nerd." The unwritten social code of our small-town high school did little to encourage camaraderie between us.

He was a rowdy guy in boots who made barely passing grades and was rumored to enjoy the affections of a "wild," out-of-town girlfriend. I was a serious-faced girl who wore dangling silver earrings and often hid a paperback novel inside an open biology textbook. We were just two of the many kids admonished by our teachers to behave, pay attention, and *grow up*.

Like many small-town daughters, I became determined as a teenager to get out of town as soon as possible. I was certain other places held excitement, mystery, and possibly even *men* not available in my hometown. I certainly didn't want to miss out on anything.

Days after graduation, I *did* leave home to attend college, and it *was* good to get away. Later, when my husband and I married, I was still afflicted with occasional bouts of wanderlust. It was I who orchestrated our move across several states.

But soon after our marriage we began to have babies and my life changed. I was like a hen who flies home to roost. Once the quest for a really good diaper bag replaced my search for the perfect collapsible suitcase, that small town began to look like a pretty good place to be.

Guided more by maternal homing instinct than by thought and planning, we moved our nest back to the community I had once been so eager to leave behind. My husband, Randy, secured a coaching position and I was hired at the local hospital. We made new "couple" friends, and I rekindled some of the friendships of my youth.

My shift in the Intensive Care Unit had begun quietly, with two of us nurses caring for only one fairly stable postoperative patient. However, within an hour we received a report from the emergency room regarding a heart-attack victim who would be coming to our unit. As we set up the monitors and turned back the bed, it was decided that my friend Tina would keep the patient we already had and I would take the new admission.

Mr. O'Donald arrived in serious condition. He was a husky man of about 55, a former smoker with a long history of heart disease. That morning his oldest son had found him slumped in the seat of his still-parked truck, where he had collapsed some time earlier. The son had called 911 and started CPR. When the paramedics arrived, they were able to stimulate the older man's heart into a ragged, unstable rhythm before they loaded him into the ambulance. Upon his arrival at the hospital, a tube was placed in Mr. O'Donald's throat and he was connected to the ventilator— a breathing machine.

The gravity of the situation was explained to the family. Because Mr. O'Donald had been without oxygen for so long, not only were his heart and lungs injured, but his brain had suffered permanent damage. He was unconscious, not responding to voices or even to pain. They needed to under-stand how critical his condition was.

The family responded in ways common to folks in this dreadful situation. Judy, his wife, cried and looked as if she herself might collapse. Daughter Susan repeatedly asked me about his temperature and voiced great and inappropriate relief when I told her he had no fever. Youngest son Mike was so shook up he refused at first to even go in and see Mr. O'Donald. He waited outside with the grandchildren.

The family was allowed at the bedside for a few minutes every two hours. I met them in the waiting room between their visits to give updates and to answer their questions. It was in the waiting room that Joel, Mr. O'Donald's oldest son, and I first recognized each other. He was red-eyed and shaky, but calm. I expressed my sadness at his dad's condition and took a few minutes to sit and talk with him.

I learned that my former classmate was no longer a rowdy kind of guy, but instead he was the minister of a downtown church. That "wild," out-of-town girlfriend had been more than just a rumor. Now the church's second-grade Sunday school teacher, she had been his wife for more than ten years.

When Joel read the "RN" on my name badge and learned I was the nurse taking care of his dad, he smiled a weak smile and commented that evidently, at some point, I must have taken biology a bit more seriously than I had in my paperback novel days.

Hours passed. Lab tests and X-rays were done. The family paced and drank endless cups of coffee. A neurologist was consulted and medications were adjusted. In late afternoon, Mr. O'Donald's cardiologist called them together and spoke as honestly and as kindly as he could.

No, Mr. O'Donald was not in pain.

Yes, his heart was very badly damaged.

No, he would not get better.

And finally, yes, the ventilator was the only thing keeping him alive.

The news was awful but by now not totally unexpected. They were a family of great dignity and faith. Though this decision was the most difficult one of their lives, they unanimously agreed to let Mr. O'Donald go. The ventilator would be turned off and their dad would be allowed to die. Neither he nor they would want a machine to keep him alive. They believed he would go on to a better place.

Mrs. O'Donald kissed her husband and told him to save her a place in heaven. Susan squeezed his hand and wept. Mike told his dad he would love him forever. Once their good-byes had been said, they left the ICU. Only Joel asked to be allowed to stay.

I drew the privacy curtains and brought in a chair. Joel moved it to the head of the bed, sat down, and began to stroke his dad's soft gray hair. The noisy ventilator was turned off and an instant, palpable quiet surrounded the two of them. I stood motionless, invisible, and silent at the foot of the bed. Joel leaned very, very close to his dying father's face, so close that his lips were almost touching the older man's ear. He drew a long steady breath and began to speak in a low and gentle voice.

The LORD is my shepherd; I shall not want.
He maketh me to lie down in green pastures;
he leadeth me beside the still waters.

I watched the screen mounted on the wall over their heads. Mr. O'Donald was still connected to the cardiac monitor, and it reflected the irregular beats of a damaged, oxygen-hungry heart. Even as I watched, I listened to Joel's whispers.

> *He restoreth my soul;*
> *he leadeth me in the paths of righteousness*
> *for his name's sake.*

The movements on the monitor grew more weak and erratic, and I calculated two- and three-second pauses between each beat.

> *Yea, though I walk through the*
> *valley of the shadow of death,*
> *I will fear no evil,*
> *for thou art with me . . .*

Finally there were no more variations of pattern on the monitor—only a straight, unwavering line. My eyes left the screen and I heard Joel's soft, steady voice complete the Twenty-third Psalm.

> *Surely goodness and mercy shall*
> *follow me all the days of my life,*
> *and I will dwell in the house*
> *of the Lord forever.*

Silence.
Goodbye, Dad.
Have a good trip.
Absently, I fingered a silver earring and wiped away a tear. I knew at this very moment that a long-ago, mostly forgotten teacher's wish had been granted.

Joel and I had grown up.

CHAPTER TWENTY-THREE

A View from the Other Side

*J*t wasn't until my own son, Russell, became a patient in the hospital where I worked that I began to understand the desperate fears and sometimes odd behaviors of patients' families.

ℒ♥ ℒ♥ ℒ♥

The letters ICU stand for Intensive Care Unit. Some facilities use the term Critical Care Unit, or CCU. Hospital personnel often refer to this area simply as "the unit." Whatever name it may be called, this area houses the most critically ill patients in the hospital. In this location very intensive nursing care is delivered, usually by *very intense* nurses.

I remember my first days of orientation in the ICU. Though I had practiced nursing for several years, I had never worked with such sick patients or such complicated equipment alongside such competent caregivers. There was always more for me learn about ventilators, special IV drips, and heart monitors. Many times I felt overwhelmed by the myriad of tubes and lines, the multiple diagnoses, and the rapidity of the changes to which I was expected to respond appropriately.

The ICU in the small hospital where I was employed held five beds. Occasionally all five were filled, but most of the time three patients would be our normal load. We cared for people with a variety of ailments, including accident victims, people having heart attacks, and postoperative patients too unstable for the regular surgical floor.

Our hospital faced a chronic nursing shortage. Sometimes there were just not enough nurses to cover all areas adequately, and some departments would be short a nurse or two. When that happened, the ICU received priority and was almost always the best-staffed location in the facility. Each nurse working in the unit was assigned only one, or at the most, two patients. Even if the unit held only one patient, two nurses were assigned. It would have been considered unsafe for the patient if a nurse were to staff the unit alone.

We ICU nurses tended to be perfectionists and took especially good care of our patients. We fed them, bathed them, and turned them in bed. We checked their cardiac outputs, calculated and adjusted their IV drip rates, and intervened when their hearts beat irregularly. We rubbed their backs, brushed their teeth, and recorded every milliliter of fluid that entered or exited their bodies.

We took *great* pride in the excellent care we gave.

At least we nurses believed we delivered good care. When it was visiting time—a mere ten minutes out of every two hours—worried family members stormed to their loved ones' bedsides. Within seconds they would call us aside and frantically inform us that their family members were—

Hot. Cold. Hungry. Thirsty. Hurting.

Please do something.

Anything.

Now.

We would smile and gently explain that while we understood their concerns, their loved ones had minute by minute been warmed, cooled, fed, watered, and pain-medicated. We would try to allay their fears, to explain the purposes of all the tubes and wires, to focus their attention on the progress their family members were making.

We were kind and polite but chagrined that anyone would even *suggest* that we, perfectionists that we were, were not taking good care of our patients.

I was in my kitchen baking brownies when the call came from my son's teacher. She had noticed a bump on Russell's back, right at the waistband of his jeans. Could I please come to the school and take a look? I was a bit irritated, but this was his teacher's first year. She was sweet and enthusiastic, but excitable and with a tendency to overreact. I expected to find a mosquito bite or some such minor skin irregularity on my son's back.

It was not a bug bite or a bruise or a scrape. Just below the top of his pants was a golfball-sized nodule. His teacher had noticed the lump when he leaned forward at his desk.

I took my son directly to our physician's office. The lump was painless and immovable, neither of which is a good sign. Fearing the lump was cancer, he sent us across town to consult with a surgeon. We saw the surgeon and were promptly directed to the hospital X-ray department for a CAT scan. The results were inconclusive. Surgery was scheduled for the following morning.

That night my husband, Randy, and I made dozens of phone calls to family and friends to tell them of Russell's surgery and to solicit their prayers. I remember feeling numb, and I could only mumble a feeble moan of a prayer.

"God, just please let him be all right."

Russell was wheeled into surgery clutching his favorite stuffed toy, a monkey named Mitchie. I sat gripping Randy's hand. Then we waited and prayed, and waited and hoped, for good news. Members of our family and a nervous roomful of our friends kept vigil with us.

Two hours passed. Mercifully, the news was good. The tumor did not appear to be cancer, a fact that was confirmed a day later by the pathology report.

Just minutes after the operation, we were allowed to see Russell as he was recovering in the ICU. He was still drowsy and he looked so small and pale.

I felt afraid and helpless.

I wanted—*needed*—to do something, to do *anything*, to help him.

Randy and I tried to rouse him.

"Russell," I asked, "are you hot? Are you cold? Are you hungry? Are you thirsty? Are you hurting?"

Only two steps away from my son's bed, three ICU nurses— my colleagues and my friends—looked up. Their eyes met mine. Each of their faces framed a knowing smile.

I tucked another blanket around my son. Then I squeezed his arm and assured him he was in *very* good hands.

He who watches over you will not slumber.

—Psalm 121:3

CHAPTER TWENTY-FOUR

Winter Blossoms

Since it is older folks who most often require medical care, I have spent many of my on-the-job hours nursing them. I find elderly patients to be both interesting and entertaining. Two women, Ruby and Pearl, embody many of the qualities I enjoy the most in older adults.

❧ ❧ ❧

Propped on the windowsill over my kitchen sink is a four-by-five inch framed sampler. A border of multicolored tulips surrounds the short saying stitched right in the center. *Bloom Where You Are Planted* is the phrase I read as I rinse my coffee cup each morning and again as I scrub my supper dishes each evening.

These five words, somewhat sloppily stitched and hastily mounted inside an inexpensive yellow frame, have "made the rounds." I completed the sampler 15 years ago and mailed it to my friend Jeanna. She and her husband Jack had just moved out of their cute but costly little house into a rundown but rent-free mobile home. This downward housing shift was made to give their budget some breathing room and to enable Jack to follow his dreams of going back to college.

Jeanna loved Jack but she *hated* that trailer. It was old, cramped, and drafty, and despite her best efforts it continued to be inhabited by a very noisy, multigenerational family of mice. Jeanna knew that she and Jack would be in the trailer for less than two years, but as she told it, this was going to be the longest two years in history.

I quickly stitched up the sampler, and when they had been living in the trailer less than a week, I mailed her a long letter and the *Bloom Where You Are Planted* stitching.

Jeanna *did* bloom. So did Jack. He even graduated. Now they look back on those mobile-home years as very happy ones.

Being married to a coach is, I suspect, a bit like serving as a minister's wife. Both coaches and preachers, even good ones, tend to wear out a town's welcome about every five years. Even though a wife *knows* it's due to happen, and even though she *tries* not to take it personally, the phrase *it's time to move on* is never easy for her to hear.

It was shortly after hearing those very words that I found myself packing to leave a town, a house, and friends I loved and would miss. I managed for the most part to put on a positive face for my husband and children, but during late-night, long-distance calls to my sympathetic friend Jeanna I poured out the feelings of my sad and fearful heart. I was encouraged when a few weeks after we had moved into our new place, the cross-stitched sampler I had sent her way arrived back in my own mailbox.

In the past ten years I have sent that same travel-weary, tulip-bordered phrase to any friend who I felt needed its message. I've requested only that the sampler continue to be passed on. I was pleased when it came back to me two weeks after we moved to our present location.

Ruby and Pearl live together in a family-run boarding home for people with Alzheimer's disease. The place where they reside is just one of a batch of newly popular homegrown facilities which provide yet another alternative to traditional nursing home care.

While Ruby and Pearl have their disease and its dementia in common, their personalities are as different as the jewels for which their mothers named them.

Ruby is both a talker and, as is common in folks with her disease, a walker. From the time she wakes up in the morning until the time she falls exhausted into bed at night, Ruby roams the rambling country house and carries on a cheerful conversation with whomever happens to be around. She wanders around the downstairs rooms, digs into dresser drawers, and pulls items out of closets. In the kitchen, if she's not watched carefully, she helpfully puts leftover food in the china cabinet and crystal goblets in the pantry.

Ruby keeps her devoted caregivers hopping because *Ruby is a woman on the move.*

Her roommate, Pearl, is a different story. Pearl is quiet and calm, plump and passive. The biggest problem the folks at the boarding home have with Pearl is getting her to change positions often enough to prevent pressure sores. Pearl is always pleasant and is the happiest of all when she's comfortably relaxed in her faded plaid recliner. She finds the chair's position in the den to be the perfect spot from which to sleep, smile, sip glasses of sweetened iced tea, and watch both the world and Ruby rush by.

My friend and nursing colleague Darleen was consulted when one of the boarding home's workers discovered a deep pressure sore on Pearl's left heel. Darleen came daily to clean and dress the wound and was greatly relieved when after three weeks of treatment it finally seemed to be healing.

Darleen's nursing visits followed a pattern. She would lay out her supplies: gloves, gauze bandages, tape, and a cup of sterile saline on the arm of Pearl's recliner. Then she would remove the old bandage, clean the wound with the saline, and apply fresh gauze and tape. The dressing change took only a few minutes. Since Pearl had almost no sensation in her foot, the treatment was painless. She was happy in her own little world and often seemed to be unaware of Darleen's presence.

Now Ruby—*Ruby* was aware of *everything* Darleen did. She chattered and rattled and picked and prowled while Pearl's dressing was being changed. Darleen zealously guarded her medical supplies from Ruby's industrious rearrangings, but otherwise tolerated the woman's interruptions and non-sensical, nonstop conversations with humor and good-natured understanding.

One morning Darleen found Pearl relaxed in her usual reclined position curiously clutching a short-stemmed cluster of silk pansies. She held the flowers not by the stems but upside down, by the blossoms. Darleen admired Pearl's flowers, wondered aloud where they had come from, and was told by a wearied worker that Ruby, enjoying a particularly energetic morning, had plucked them from the hall table. Never one to do a job halfway, Ruby had dismantled the entire arrangement and generously distributed the artificial botanical plunder evenly among the home's residents.

Darleen chuckled as she laid out the supplies for Pearl's treatment. She was about to remove the old dressing when she realized she had left a necessary roll of tape in her car. Finding Ruby to be safely occupied eating a snack in the kitchen, Darleen sprinted out to her car to get the tape.

Darleen returned to Pearl, knelt at her feet, and removed the wound's gauze. She inspected Pearl's heel for signs of infection, saw none, and reached for the cup of sterile saline she would use to clean the wound.

The cup was not there.

Darleen straightened up and looked again. Perhaps she had set it on the floor beside the recliner.

Not there.

Maybe she had neglected to get the saline out of her supply bag.

Not there either.

Had she left the tape *and* the saline in her car?

No.

"Where," Darleen asked in exasperation, "is that cup of saline? I *know* I set it right here."

Ruby, the obvious culprit, had not moved from her spot at the table.

Pearl, who by this time had begun to snore, did not offer an explanation either. Finally Darleen glanced at the woman's lap. Pearl was still holding the silk pansies, but she had turned them upright. The flower's stems, judged to be *very* thirsty, had been plunged into the mysteriously missing cup of saline!

Pearl and Ruby are women who used to know all about growing flowers. In their younger, more lucid days, they tended beautiful beds of annuals and gently competed with each other for prizes at local garden shows. Before coming down with Alzheimer's disease, either one of them could have told you how some flowers (like zinnias) require lots of sunshine, while others (like impatiens) thrive in heavy shade. They could have told you that sunflowers seem to bloom forever, and warned you that the beauty of daylilies is fleeting.

Pearl and Ruby learned long ago that pink petunias and gold marigolds and red salvias are beautiful in the spring and on through the summer, but that they, like most annual flowers, die down at the first frost of winter. Pansies, they both knew, are one of the few varieties of flowers that are at their brightest and boldest when winter sets in.

At this stage in her disease Pearl can't tell a silk flower from a real one, and lately Ruby is better at tearing things up than at tending them. Still, like the frost-hardy pansies they remind me of, well into the winters of their lives they remain both bright and bold.

It's true that Ruby and Pearl are increasingly forgetful these days. Neither of them can prepare a flower bed or cook a meal. But there is one thing they do better than many of us healthy folks: Ruby and Pearl are some of the best folks around when it comes to taking the advice that's propped on my windowsill. I'd say Ruby and Pearl are still blooming away.

They will still bear fruit in old age,
they will stay fresh and green.

—PSALM 92:14

CHAPTER TWENTY-FIVE

A Carpenter Called Buddy

I am frequently inspired and humbled at the lengths people go in their attempts to care for their hurting family and friends. The services of these unpaid caregivers are to me love made visible. I saw with my own eyes such visible love in the care that Otis, Darlie, and Buddy gave to a sick, cranky woman named Hannah.

❧ ❧ ❧

She had no family, having outlived them all. She was old, eccentric, and ornery. Hannah was very sick, but she refused to go to the hospital.

It started with a blister on her chin. She put kerosene, pork grease, and aloe vera juice on it. Hannah alternately ignored it, and picked at it, and when it got bigger and began to hurt, she finally consulted the Rural Health Clinic doctor.

Dr. Gerard was kind but blunt: Hannah needed an oncologist. The lesion was a cancerous tumor which was too large to remove in the office. She would need follow-up care, probably chemotherapy.

Dr. Gerard was good at treating sore throats, diagnosing gout, and stitching up cut fingers, but a cancerous tumor was out of his league. Hannah must go to Houston, where the finest medical specialists would evaluate her case and provide the most effective, cutting-edge treatments available. He would make all the arrangements and could probably get her an appointment before the end of the week.

"No way," was Hannah's response to his recommendation. "I am not going to Houston. I know all about those Houston hospitals. My cousin went there and never did come back. People die in those places! No sirree, I will stay right in my own house and continue with my own remedies, thank you very much."

Dr. Gerard tried to talk to Hannah, tried his best to reason with her, but there would be no reasoning. Her mind was made up.

To say that Hannah was hard to get along with would be stating it mildly. In her old age she was harmless enough, but as a younger woman she had feared no one and had sometimes been downright mean. She especially hated children, dogs, and preachers.

Every time her neighbor's poodle wandered into her yard to take a sniff, she called the dogcatcher.

She posted a NO TRESPASSING sign in her yard. When an unsuspecting, not-yet-able-to-read Girl Scout cookie peddler rang her doorbell, she invited the girl in and gave her a chocolate-flavored laxative.

The Mount Zion Baptist Church once called a new minister, a sandy-haired young man fresh out of seminary. When Brother James and his new bride called on Hannah, she told him that all preachers were money-grabbing frauds and to never come back. He didn't.

Through the years Hannah pretty much managed to alienate everyone who knew her. Everyone, that is, except Otis, Darlie, and her best friend Buddy. None of them could say why they cared about the unpleasant old woman—they just did. Sometimes they were exasperated or embarrassed by her behavior. Sometimes they admired her feistiness in the face of something as serious as cancer.

For whatever reason, they loved Hannah.

The tumor grew larger and Hannah grew weaker. She could no longer leave her house and depended on Otis, Darlie, and Buddy to tend to her needs. From the bed she had made on the couch, Hannah ordered the three volunteers around like she was their queen and they were her unworthy subjects.

Otis did her errands, bought her groceries, and came over every morning to cook her oatmeal. Otis was a good cook, but he never quite got the oatmeal just right. It was always too thick or too thin. Hannah would give him money to shop for groceries, then insisted on counting the change and checking every receipt to be sure he hadn't pocketed a penny or two.

Darlie was a nurse. She cleaned and bandaged the vile wound and tried to get Hannah to take her medication. She came at six o'clock every evening, but Hannah insisted on calling her at work or at home, sometimes a dozen times a day.

"Hannah, you've just got to quit calling me all day. My boss and my husband are both tired of it," Darlie pleaded.

Hannah got so mad at Darlie's request that she didn't let her into the house three evenings in a row.

Buddy, a carpenter, was Hannah's favorite person in the whole world and she let *him* do *everything* else. He brought her steak finger baskets from Dairy Queen, repaired her leaky toilet, and changed her soiled sheets. When Hannah got scared at two in the morning, it was Buddy she called. When the pain made her cry, it was Buddy she wanted to hold her hand. Hannah never once got mad at Buddy, even when he chided her to be nicer to Otis and Darlie.

In time Otis, Darlie, and Buddy were forced to make a difficult decision. Hannah's condition had deteriorated to the point where the three could no longer provide as much care as she needed. I was called upon to help them with possible nursing-home placement.

Buddy had prepared Hannah by telling her I was coming. He sat next to her the entire time it took for me to perform my assessment and evaluation. I asked Hannah some questions and filled out some of the necessary paperwork.

At that point Hannah began to tire, and she complained that her feet hurt. I bent to massage them.

"No, I want Buddy to do it. He knows how to do it," she moaned.

I watched as Buddy, sweat-stained and still wearing his grimy work boots and tool belt, drew a pan of warm water. He helped Hannah sit up, then knelt in front of her and gently bathed her scaly, aching feet. After a soothing soak, he dried her feet with a threadbare towel and tenderly rubbed them with lavender-scented cream.

Hannah closed her eyes and sighed contentedly.

Until this moment I had never laid eyes on Buddy, but observing him take such tender care of Hannah reminded me of a friend I had known for a very long time. As I looked upon the intimate scene, I recalled the story of the time my friend, also a carpenter, washed the feet of a few folks.

I strongly suspect that Buddy and my Carpenter Friend have met.

I was sick and you looked after me.

—MATTHEW 25:36

CHAPTER TWENTY-SIX

Burnout

I enjoy my work. Certainly there are days I wish I could just turn off the alarm and sleep another hour. Sometimes I long to just spend the day puttering at home, but once I greet my first patient I am usually ready and eager to begin my workday. However, there was a time when I, like many of my colleagues, experienced a period of career burnout. Aid during my recovery from this pit of near-despair came from a surprising source.

✿ ✿ ✿

I found myself tired and irritable instead of energetic and positive. Going to sleep at night was difficult and waking up in the morning was even harder. When I did sleep, I had wild nightmares about sick patients whom I had somehow forgotten to care for. I was eating too much and watching more hours of mindless late-night television than I care to admit.

As the supervisor of a home health agency, I was faced with lots of touchy situations and difficult decisions. I found that events I once saw as "creative challenges" began to loom before me as insurmountable problems.

When a patient's daughter complained because I arrived ten minutes later than she expected, I held my tongue, but I was frightened by the fierce anger I felt within. After the owner of the agency questioned a staffing decision I had made I burst into a torrent of tears.

I forgot important paperwork deadlines, and my handwritten nurse's notes became barely legible. Twice I drove miles to patients' homes only to have to turn right around and return to the office for a forgotten bag of vital medical supplies.

My best nursing buddy, Darleen, intervened. She came into my office, shut the door, looked me in the eye, and made a loving diagnosis:

"Annette, I think you're having a problem with burnout. Sooner or later everyone does. You need to have some time alone. Take a little break."

She was right. I was more than just tired, and I was way beyond stressed-out. Though I was accustomed to and even enjoyed being the giver of my abilities, talents, and education, I had to admit that right then I was all "gived out."

My tank was out of gas.

My cup was dry.

I was a healer in need of healing.

Though I knew I needed to take some time off, our family's finances and the agency's heavy caseload would not allow me to do so. The afternoon Darleen confronted me, I locked my office door and spent the better part of two hours talking with her. She listened and listened and listened. She held me, hugged me, wiped my tears, and prayed for me.

I took Friday off in order to give myself a long weekend. The phone didn't get answered and the laundry went undone. My family granted my request for some time alone.

When I returned to the office on Monday, I was rested and ready to work, but still fragile and forgetful. Several out-of-town patients needed to be seen, so I planned my route, gathered my supplies, and hit the road.

In the Deep East Texas forest where I live, every fall for about three weeks we experience an onslaught—swarms of small winged insects. The locals call them "love bugs." But residents don't love these critters at all. On the contrary, they drive us crazy. When we step outside our houses the bugs fly into our eyes and ears, and when we drive, their splattered bodies cover our windshields and sometimes even clog our radiators. The remains of these insects are so sticky that we have to scrub and even scrape them off with strong cleaners and metal blades.

Unfortunately, my episode of burnout collided with the love bugs' heyday. By the time I had driven the 30 miles to Mrs. Crowsen's house, I could barely see the road in front of my van. I tried to clean the windshield, but after a few anemic squirts my vehicle's reservoir of cleaning fluid ran dry. All I had with me was an old towel and a few baby wipes. After driving into Mrs. Crowsen's driveway, I tried in vain to clean the opaque bodies off my windshield before they dried. But I just made the mess worse.

Mr. Crowsen was working in his garden wearing his usual faded overalls and straw hat, and was so absorbed in his work that he barely acknowledged my arrival. I yelled a greeting to him and made my way up the steps and into the house to check on his diabetic wife. Her blood sugar reading was high and she had a slight fever. After phoning her doctor, I relayed his careful instructions and told her I would be back in the morning.

Mr. Crowsen returned my goodbye wave but kept right on hoeing his beans. I buckled myself back into my van and pulled out of the gravel driveway.

Ten miles down the road it suddenly occurred to me that my windshield was clean. Crystal clear, in fact. Not only was the windshield clean, but all the windows and mirrors had been scrubbed until they gleamed. While I had been inside caring for his wife, elderly Mr. Crowsen had been outside caring for me.

When I realized what he had done, a tear slid down my cheek. I have been the grateful recipient of grand acts of kindness in my life, but for some reason this gesture on this particular day moved me beyond words.

Mrs. Crowsen's blood sugar returned to normal and her fever went down. The nursing visit I made that Monday made little long-term difference in her life. I think she probably would have improved with or without my intervention.

My life, however, was changed in some small way that fall morning. Not only did Mr. Crowsen clean my windshield so that I could see clearly to drive, but he cleaned up my vision so I could see joy again.

There are rare days when the earthly becomes heavenly. This was one of those days.

I had a full tank of gas.

My cup was full to the brim.

I was a healer on her way to being healed.

My cup overflows.

—Psalm 23:5

TWENTY-SEVEN

Lizard Lady

umor often finds its way into a hospital setting. In even the most difficult of situations, laughter can provide a welcome diversion. My patient Faye was a master trickster and a lover of practical jokes. She taught me the value of enjoying the lighter side of life.

✿ ✿ ✿

When Faye's next-door neighbor, Tom, bought a new car, she trotted across her yard to get a good look at it. Tom was really proud of the vehicle and showed Faye all its newfangled features. He pointed out the comfortable interior, demonstrated the fancy sound system, and went into great detail about the car's energy efficiency. Feeling a need to justify what he admitted to himself was a slightly extravagant expenditure, Tom elaborated on what excellent gas mileage he was sure his new vehicle would get. Since he commuted 15 miles to work each day, this car would save him a lot of money.

Faye indulgently admired Tom's car, and even let him take her for a cautious spin around the block. They stopped for coffee, and over hot apple pie she agreed with Tom that

141

he had certainly bought a wonderful car and that with his great expected gas mileage he had *really* gotten a great deal.

That night Tom parked his new car under the carport, went to bed, and slept soundly, enjoying dreams of long Sunday drives in the country and speedy, convenient trips to the city.

That night Faye, an expert practical joker, went to bed, but *she* couldn't sleep. Her mind was too busy hatching a plan.

The next day she retrieved a gas can from a garage shelf, carted it to the Texaco station down the street, and filled it up. That night Faye stayed up late waiting for Tom to go to bed. Keeping an eye on his house from her kitchen window, she waited for his bedroom light to go out. Finally, when she was sure he had retired for the night, she slipped out of her house, retrieved the gas can from her trunk, and trespassed right onto his property. Carefully she sneaked past his well-lit backdoor and slipped into the the open carport. Groping in the dark, it took her a minute to locate, by touch alone, the gas tank on Tom's new car. Stealthily she unscrewed the cap, shakily raised the heavy gas can, and completely filled the car's tank.

Once her mission was accomplished, Faye sprinted across the yard and back to her own house. She placed the empty gas can in her car trunk, went back inside, washed her hands, and went to bed.

The next day, none the wiser, Tom made his regular 15 mile commute to work. He didn't mind the drive so much, secure in the fact that his newly purchased transportation made the trip both comfortable and economical.

The next night Faye waited for Tom to go to bed and then repeated her nocturnal escapade. Once again she topped off the level of gasoline in the tank of his car.

Faye returned to fill Tom's car's gas tank the next night. And the next. And the next. She continued to make her sneaky visits to her unsuspecting neighbor's carport every night for a month.

For the first few days Tom was as pleased as punch to find that his new car *seemed* to use *no* gasoline. He bragged to his coworkers and casually mentioned it twice to Faye.

It was all she could do not to burst into laughter when after five days Tom began scratching his head in wonder at the fact that the car's gas gauge never moved from FULL. He had expected to get good gas mileage, but this was unbeliev-able! After the first week he was increasingly curious about his car's fuel-efficiency phenomenon. After two weeks he was curious to the point of being agitated. Finally, after a month with *no* trips to the gas station, poor Tom was ready to take his car right back to the dealer and demand to be told what in the world was wrong with the vehicle.

Faye was forced to confess her crime.

Tom was at first disbelieving, then rather embarrassed. In the end, though, he was most tickled at Faye's prank, even if the joke was on him.

Faye, expert trickster that she was, considered this fuel-efficiency plot to have been one of her finest.

Faye was a patient in the ICU when I met her. She had been diagnosed with congestive heart failure, a condition characterized by shortness of breath, weakness, swelling, and an irregular, inefficient heartbeat. Faye had suffered several heart attacks over the years and her heart muscle was badly damaged. Her condition was serious, and at age 78 she had made the decision not to be connected to life support should her heart stop beating or her breathing cease.

The layout of our hospital's ICU offered little in the way of privacy. Individual beds were separated by curtains, and unless we nurses were working with a particular patient, we kept them pulled open so we could keep an eye on each bed from our station. The unit's layout meant that not only could we nurses see and hear everything our patients did and said, but that our patients, if they were alert, were able to see and hear practically everything we did and said as well.

Though ICU is a serious place, and though ICU nurses take their jobs seriously, there is usually room for some humor on the job. That morning Faye, who was enjoying one of her rare "good" days, overheard nurses Janet and Elaine concocting a plot to scare the wits out of Beth.

Beth, the unit's beloved supervisor, was known to be a self-confident, gutsy kind of gal. She had no qualms about traveling cross-country all alone, and once she shot at an intruder trying to break into her house. Beth was one of the bravest women I knew, but there was one thing we all knew she was afraid of.

Beth was afraid of lizards.

Big ones, little ones, green ones, brown ones—it didn't matter, because Beth was afraid of every one of them. Just talking about lizards in front of Beth made her palms sweat. Seeing one reduced her to a quivery state resembling melted gelatin.

Janet had managed, that very morning, to borrow her six-year-old son Jake's very realistic-looking rubber lizard. Naturally, as any good prankster would have done, Janet brought it to work with her. She and Elaine were now trying to decide how best to utilize this delicate instrument of fright.

"Let's put it in her lunch sack."

"No. Tuck it into her desk drawer."

"How about just putting it in her chair?"

Faye overheard them.

Could she please, oh *please*, get in on the prank? She *loved* jokes, and just listening to them talk, she had already thought of a much better plan.

Janet and Elaine agreed to go along with Faye's plot.

When Beth returned from lunch, Faye adopted a decidedly pained look and called Beth to her bedside. Would Beth *please* check her IV site? It was hurting. *Badly*.

Of course she would. Beth first washed her hands, then moved to Faye's bedside and pulled back the sheet to expose the hurting hand. There, tucked in the bed, was the lizard.

Beth screamed and Faye just laughed and laughed. Eventually Beth had a good laugh too, though she warned Janet and Elaine that she *would* be getting them back when the time came for their next employee evaluations. Faye couldn't remember when she had enjoyed anything as much as the look on Beth's face when she saw that lizard.

That continued to be a good day for Faye. She felt well enough to tell the lizard story over and over to anyone who stood still long enough to hear it. Thanks to her, within just a few hours the whole hospital had learned of Janet and Elaine's escapade and of Beth's predictable reaction. Faye recounted the tale to her doctor, to the lab technician, and to the attendant who mopped the floor. Since they all knew about Beth's reptilian fears, the story had them all in stitches.

When Faye's children and grandchildren came to visit that evening, she told them her lizard story. They shared in her laughter and reminisced about all of the past Faye-inflicted pranks they had been the unsuspecting victims of. When their short visit was over, they playfully chided her to behave herself and go easy on us nurses. Then they kissed her and told her they would see her in the morning.

Faye had a fairly easy night but woke the next morning short of breath and complaining that her chest hurt. She was extremely restless and agitated. We medicated her, rubbed her back, and made her as comfortable as was possible. I phoned her family at home and told them Faye was not having a good day. They should not delay coming to the hospital.

Later that afternoon, with her family holding hands around her hospital bed, and as she had requested—with no medical intervention—Faye died.

We did our best to support the family in their grief. Though they, and we, had known her death was imminent, it had surprised us all because she had felt so well the day before. It had been easy for us, and I would like to believe for Faye, to forget for a few hours just how sick she was. However,

I did worry that perhaps yesterday's levity had made the situation more difficult for her family.

My fears were relieved when Faye's daughter and son called Janet and Elaine aside. They thanked them over and over for bringing laughter to their mother's last day and for letting her in on their joke.

They knew it was just how Faye would have wanted to go out—not in a blaze of glory but in a trail of laughter.

> *Even in laughter the heart may ache,*
> *and joy may end in grief.*

—Proverbs 14:13

CHAPTER TWENTY-EIGHT

In the Eye of the Beholder

*M*y grandma lives in a nursing home. Her living there helps me have greater empathy for the feelings which the families of my patients experience. An incident involving the treatment my grandma received taught me a great deal about what it means to become a loving caregiver.

❧ ❧ ❧

The nursing home where my grandmother lives is a very good one. The facility is equipped with comfortable resident rooms, tastefully decorated living areas, a well-equipped physical therapy suite, and a sunny cafeteria. The staff includes qualified nurses and compassionate, courteous aides.

Grandma likes it there. She enjoys visiting with the friends and neighbors who live on her hall and participating in the variety of social events organized by the facility's activity director. She likes the food and she likes her room. Looking after her bedfast roommate—making sure the woman stays covered up—allows her to continue her lifelong habit of caring for others.

Though Grandma and her friends appreciate all of the nursing home's amenities, it is the beauty shop that does the most to prompt their good spirits and to spark their feelings of well-being. Every Wednesday the ladies eagerly sign up to receive their weekly beauty boosts. Professional hair stylists provide shampoos and sets, and friendly volunteers polish the ladies' fingernails in shades ranging from the palest of pinks to the raciest of reds. The shop offers a full range of services, and about every six weeks, in addition to her weekly wash and set, Grandma gets a haircut and has a color rinse applied.

Neither Grandma's vision nor her coordination is as good as it used to be, and she is unable to do much of her own grooming. She requires a hairdo that is both attractive and low-maintenance. After experimenting with several looks, she, in consultation with her hairdresser and with my mom, has decided that her thin, fine hair looks best when styled in face-framing curls. Since her hair is naturally straight, about every three months she gets a permanent wave. It's a bit expensive and time-consuming, but worth every penny.

My mother, who visits the nursing home almost every evening, recently noticed that though it had been only two weeks since her last permanent, Grandma's hair was looking straight and flat. Instead of being flatteringly fluffed and poufed, her hair was parted down the middle and slicked flat against her head. The look was *most* unattractive.

"Who," Mom gingerly asked Grandma, "fixed your hair this morning?"

"Hon," Grandma replied, "there's a new girl working my hall. Her name is Libby. She helped me get dressed this morning. She fixed my hair too. Do you like it?"

Mom, wanting Grandma to look her best, told her the hairdo needed just a *little* touching up. She got out the brush and curling iron, and in a very few minutes, she had Grandma's hair looking pretty again—fluffed up and curly.

Grandma chattered on and on about the new aide. Libby had two cute little girls—she had seen their pictures—and a "no-account" husband who was out of a job. Libby used to work at an elementary school, but she liked working at the nursing home much better. Libby liked old John Wayne movies and pink roses and her favorite dessert was chocolate cream pie.

Over the next few weeks Mom heard more and more about Libby, but since she worked the morning shift and Mom visited in the evenings, the two never met. Mom did, however, continue to redo Grandma's hair every day that Libby was on duty. During these redos she learned about the smallest details of Libby's life.

"Libby has beans coming up in her garden."

"Libby's mother is in the hospital. The poor soul is suffering with gout."

"Libby's daughter, Julie, received a good citizenship award at school."

"Libby is getting new carpet for her living room."

Mom was happy Grandma liked Libby so much. She just wished the aide would quit brushing her hairdo out. Grandma has always taken pride in her appearance, and Mom is determined to do what she can to help her mother-in-law look as nice as possible for as long as possible. It pains Mom to see some of the home's formerly dignified residents looking unkempt in their old age. She makes sure Grandma has pretty housedresses, sturdy slippers, and sweet-smelling powders and lotions.

It really began to bother her to arrive evening after evening to find Grandma unattractively flat-haired, and she continued to spend a good part of her visits patiently repairing Libby's hairbrush-inflicted damage.

Finally Mom decided enough was enough. She would make a point to be at the nursing home in the morning. She planned to meet this Libby person and politely but firmly tell her to please *quit brushing out Grandma's curls*.

Bright and early the next day, Mom arrived in time to speak with the aide. She had greeted Grandma and stepped momentarily into the bathroom when a stunning young black woman burst into the room. Mom watched, not hiding exactly, but nevertheless unseen, as the woman swooped Grandma into a generous bear hug and planted a loud kiss on her cheek.

"How's my very favorite resident today? Did you sleep well last night, Sweetheart? Are you ready to get dressed? Let's find something really pretty to wear."

Grandma, delighted to see her friend, returned the hug.

Mom quietly watched as Libby patiently helped Grandma put on fresh underclothes and slip into her favorite housedress. The young woman searched high and low for a certain pair of earrings Grandma wanted to wear and sat right down on the floor in order to put Grandma's shoe on without hurting her sore toe.

Once Grandma was dressed, Libby helped her apply rose-colored lipstick and began to brush her hair. Very carefully she made a center part and neatly brushed the sides and back down very straight and smooth. Over and over she made the gentle strokes, checking first one side, then the other, and then continued to brush until there was not one curl left.

Observing them from the bathroom, Mom watched as Libby lovingly and deliberately brushed Grandma's hair into a style exactly like her own, a style that on her beautiful face was most youthful and becoming. When Libby was finished, she and Grandma sported identical hairstyles.

"There now." She patted Grandma on the cheek. "Don't you look pretty as a picture. Are you ready for breakfast?"

My grandma, a wrinkled old white woman, looked into the young toffee-colored woman's eyes and beamed like sunshine.

Finally Mom stepped out of the bathroom and greeted Libby. "I'm so happy to finally meet you. I want to tell you how much I appreciate the way you take such good care of Grandma. And I just love the way you've fixed her hair. It looks lovely."

And it did.

Even the very hairs of your head are all numbered.

—MATTHEW 10:30

CHAPTER TWENTY-NINE

Blood Sisters

I've always believed that people who volunteer are healthier and happier than those who don't.

My friend Esther's benefactor, Alice, is a dramatic example of how much the giving of oneself can improve a life.

❦ ❦ ❦

Alice and Jeff's new house was the talk of the town.

"British half-timber style," explained their English-born architect.

"Impressive," gushed their envious friends.

"*Five bathrooms?*" questioned Jeff's depression-survivor parents.

Alice had always hoped to live in a two-story house. With four bedrooms, five bathrooms, an office, a playroom, and a formal living room and dining room, it was larger than any of their friends' homes. The showy stucco-and-brick house stared down from its position on the summit of a wooded hill. Professional landscaping and a long curving driveway added to its grand beauty.

How could a young couple afford such a home?

Jeff, who Alice had married right out of college, was a financial prodigy. He was a hard worker but was also what his colleagues called "one lucky son of a gun." Practically every investment venture he attempted seemed to turned to gold overnight. At age 32, Jeff had made his first million. He was an energetic, handsome, and attentive husband.

Alice was pretty and outwardly pleasant. She was claimed by a large circle of friends and was a member of three social clubs and an officer in the PTA. Alice's reputation was that of a good hostess. She and Jeff invited friends to their home almost every weekend, and were regularly invited in return.

Early in their marriage the couple was blessed with two children—a boy and a girl. Joshua and Jennifer, at ages six and eight, were cute, easygoing, well-behaved children. Both made good grades in school. Joshua was athletic and Jennifer was artistic. They were popular with their teachers and well-liked by their classmates.

Alice and Jeff had it all.

At least that's what their friends and family said.

Because Alice was mostly able to hide it, only Jeff and Alice's sister, Liz, knew that in fact what Alice actually had was *depression*.

She knew it made no sense to them. It didn't even make sense to her. But the apathy and sadness and feelings of worthlessness she had struggled with for more than a year were as real as the fever and achiness that Jeff experienced when he came down with the flu.

Alice couldn't just shake off her symptoms. She *wanted* to feel better. She really did.

What should she do?

Jeff thought that buying new furniture would lift her spirits.

Her family physician, elderly Dr. Stevens, advised her to have a baby.

Her sister helpfully suggested a hysterectomy.

Alice tried anything and everything to get over the depression—except the baby and the hysterectomy—and she gave strong consideration to both of those suggestions. She volunteered at her children's school, joined an exercise class, and took a college course. She threw herself into decorating the new house, cooking gourmet meals, and planning the flower beds. Obediently she took medication that made her eyes scratchy and her throat dry.

Still, it was a struggle to get out of bed every morning. She hid in the bathroom and cried several times a day, lost her appetite, and sometimes didn't fall asleep until two or three in the morning.

Jeff couldn't believe Alice would even consider donating blood.

"You're *already* worn out all the time," he protested. "It will take too much out of you. I don't think it's a good idea, Honey."

Her squeamish sister, Liz, agreed. Just thinking about the process made her feel light-headed and slightly nauseous.

So Alice forgot about it.

Or she tried. But something in the church bulletin request continued to tug at her. Esther, a 50-year-old grandmother, had recently been diagnosed with leukemia. She needed blood.

Lots of it.

Soon.

As Alice understood it, Esther, who had a rare blood type, was undergoing an experimental treatment. She needed someone to give a component of his or her blood on a regular basis for an unknown length of time. All of Esther's family had been tested, but none of their blood was a suitable match. In an attempt to locate compatible blood, Esther's family had pleaded for members of the church and community to be tested. They just *had* to find *someone* who could serve as a donor.

What must it be like to need something so desperately and not be able to get it? Without mentioning it to anyone, Alice dialed the number listed in the bulletin and made an appointment at the blood center to be tested. She wouldn't qualify anyway, so what would it hurt?

Alice received both a call and a request exactly 12 hours after being tested. Of the 86 people who had tried to be Esther's donor, only *her* blood had proved compatible.

"We need you to come to the blood center today." In fact, the voice on the phone was more commanding than requesting. "One o'clock?"

"But . . . I hadn't really planned . . . you mean . . . today?"

"Today. One o'clock," the voice repeated.

So Alice became Esther's regular blood donor.

After eating her required protein-rich lunch, Alice drove to the center, where her blood pressure and temperature were checked by a technician. When they were found to be normal, she was settled into a comfortable recliner. She squeezed her eyes shut while her arms were swabbed with iodine and punctured with large bore needles. Two sites were necessary. Alice's blood left her right arm and was processed through a filter that removed the needed part of her blood. After filtering, the blood flowed back into her left arm. The whole process—giving, filtering, and getting back—took between four and five hours.

The most unpleasant part of donation was after the filtering, when the blood began to flow back into her body; it had cooled enough to give her the shakes. She would begin to tremble and shiver, and the blood bank attendants would heap piles of oven-warmed blankets over her. They would tenderly tuck them around her shoulders and under her feet, and they would feed her snacks: cookies and crackers, warm milk and juice. If she felt sleepy, they dimmed the lights and lowered their voices.

Since Alice received her blood back, missing only one of its components, the normal time required between donations did not apply. Alice could safely donate every two weeks.

And she did.

The easing of her sadness was subtle at first—in fact, barely noticeable. Then Alice began to realize that after each half-day spent at the blood center she felt better . . . stronger . . . lighter. Her appetite improved and her energy level increased.

So she kept doing it.

Jeff chided her and worried over her, but didn't try to stop her.

Liz rolled her eyes and said she didn't want to hear about it.

Alice looked forward to donating. She concentrated on her blood as it flowed out her right arm, through the tubing, to the filter, back through the tubing, and to her left arm. As the filter collected the life-extending white blood component, it also seemed to Alice to be collecting and filtering out her depression.

After three months of giving her blood, Alice truly felt better. Her husband and sister saw that she had grown stronger and healthier.

After three months of receiving Alice's blood, Esther felt better too. She is my friend, and I saw that she had grown stronger and healthier.

It has been many years since Alice read about Esther in the church bulletin. The type of blood transfusions that Esther required have long since been replaced by more effective treatments.

Alice and Esther, who hardly knew each other before Esther got sick, are now so close that some people assume they are kin. When asked about their family ties, the two women smile, wrap their arms around each other's waists, and explain with twinkling eyes that they are in fact sisters.

Sisters by blood and by love.

It is the blood that makes atonement for one's life.

—LEVITICUS 17:11

CHAPTER THIRTY

Some Can See Stars

*T*here are several teachers and numerous home-
makers among my ancestors, but so far as I
know I am the first female in my family to
become a nurse. I do have an aunt by marriage, the wife of
my mother's brother, who has practiced nursing for many
years. We enjoy sharing "war stories," and she is both a friend
and an example to me.

♥ ♥ ♥

Just before I turned 13, my family and I traveled to
Minnesota to spend the holidays with my Aunt Norma and
Uncle Rodger. We Texans rarely see snow, so it was a real
treat for us to enjoy a white Christmas.

I have many memories of that particular trip, but one of
my favorites is of the marking of my early January birthday.
Treated to an elegant "adults only" dinner at my aunt and
uncle's favorite celebratory restaurant, I remember ordering a
dish called Lobster Thermador. I had no idea what I might be
served, but I knew I liked the sophisticated way the words
sounded when I spoke them to our white-gloved waiter.

The highlight of the evening for me was when the restaurant's tuxedo-jacketed strolling string quartet surrounded our

candelit table and serenaded me with a moving rendition of Happy Birthday. My Aunt Norma, wanting to record the moment on film, snapped a quick photo. Unfortunately, for just an instant the lead violinist of the group, temporarily blinded by Norma's well-aimed flash camera, lost his poise and his place. The unexpected screeching sound that his violin made lives on only in my memory, but the sight of his startled though ever-dignified face is held captive forever between the pages of my photo album.

Aunt Norma and I stay in touch, and recently I shared a catchy phrase with her. She liked the phrase as much as I did, and someday I hope to stitch it onto a pillow or have it penned and framed and give it to her as a gift. The saying goes like this:

We can't all be stars.
But we can all twinkle.

Aunt Norma became a nurse when she was a young woman. She enjoyed her work, and though she practiced in several different medical facilities, she was especially satisfied with her position in a nursing home. Through the years she realized she had always felt most fulfilled when she worked with the elderly. Not only was serving the aged her love, it was also her talent.

After Norma's children were grown, she returned to the university. She studied hard and became an expert in the field of aging and in the management of its associated problems and challenges. Norma's background in nursing and her specialized training in geriatrics gave her excellent qualifications. Just after completing her degree, she was hired to oversee a newly opened adult daycare center designed for those who exhibit the symptoms of Alzheimer's disease.

For the families of these forgetful folks, the center is a godsend. While their loved ones are cared for in a safe, nurturing environment during the day, their primary care-givers are able to work and rest and tend to all the myriad details necessary to sustain busy modern life. Though not the answer for every Alzheimer's patient, the adult daycare center Norma oversees does provide a workable solution for many.

The progression of Alzheimer's disease is as unpredictable as is its onset. Some patients lose their memories and reasoning abilities very quickly, while others remain at a more stable level of functioning for months or occasionally even for years. Memory remains much a mystery, and no one can explain how a woman with Alzheimer's disease can forget how to feed herself but remain able to arrange the spices in her kitchen cupboard in perfect alphabetical order. It is heartbreaking for a wife when her husband no longer recognizes her, and it is baffling when the same husband, retired for ten years, insists on dressing for work every day.

Norma has a real compassion and a genuine love for the men and women she cares for. She greets them each morning and eases them out of their coats; if they need help, she feeds them their breakfasts. She listens to them, talks to them, calms them, and gently redirects them when they behave inappropriately. In describing her work to me, Aunt Norma is quick to assure me the job isn't perfect. She gets tired and discouraged, and just like her sometimes-cranky clients, there are mornings when she really would rather stay home.

On those difficult days, Norma calls to mind a memorable scene involving one of her dearest clients. Only a few days after she was settled into her new position at the center, Norma learned that her favorite violinist from her favorite restaurant was also a client. She was at first saddened to observe his absent gaze, but later thrilled when he took his violin out of its case and began to play.

She recalls how she involuntarily stopped what she was doing and stood as if rooted to the floor, transfixed by the beautiful sounds of his instrument. Norma remembers how, when her friend was finished, she thanked him for the lovely music, and how, once she was alone, she thanked God that this sweet man's gift was, for today at least, still intact.

More than most folks I know, my Aunt Norma recognizes stars that truly twinkle.

The morning stars sang together
and all the angels shouted for joy.

—JOB 38:7

—— ❧ ——

PART FIVE

*Lessons
Learned*

—— ❧ ——

CHAPTER THIRTY-ONE

One Lucky Guy

I am blessed with a very optimistic personality. I am a positive thinker and generally expect good things in my life. When I met Ethan, however, I witnessed a completely elevated level of bright-eyed optimism.

♥ ♥ ♥

When Ethan graduated from high school, he was lavished with gifts from family and friends. Almost every day in May the mail brought something to add to the ever-growing stack of goodies on the dining room table. He received luggage from his grandparents, a briefcase from his great-aunt Liz, four leather wallets, two nail-care kits, and five engraved key chains from various relatives and family friends.

Ethan was also "gifted" with money. Lots of it. All totaled, by the end of June the shoebox in his sock drawer held $645.

Everyone had ideas about how free-spirited Ethan should spend his graduation money. His younger sister Amy was sure he should use the money to buy a new sound system. His parents urged him to put the funds toward a computer to use at college. His best friend, Joe, located a totally cool used motorcycle. He was almost positive Ethan could talk the owner down to $600.

The question was on everyone's mind. "Ethan, what are you going to buy with all that money?"

Ethan researched sound systems. The salesman said digital was the latest in musical technology. He could even purchase, at very little additional cost, an extended warranty for any system he bought.

Ethan talked to the guy at the computer store and priced various components. His parents volunteered to chip in the extra money he would need to get a model he could use at college.

Ethan test-drove the used motorcycle. The owner offered it to him for $650. Joe had an extra helmet that Ethan could have for nothing.

After carefully considering all his options, Ethan bought an aquarium.

"An *aquarium*?" repeated his younger sister Amy.

"An *aquarium*?" his parents chided.

"You bought a *fish tank*?" Joe was disbelieving.

Not just *any* aquarium, but a four-foot-long aquarium. Not top of the line, since even 600 dollars wouldn't buy top of the line, but an absolutely gorgeous tank, landscaped with a variety of gracefully swaying water plants and inhabited by a blinding assortment of brilliantly colored aquatic creatures of various sizes and shapes.

An aquarium was what Ethan wanted, and in a move characteristic of his unconventional and lighthearted personality, an aquarium was what he bought. That fall, after some dramatic and slightly damp maneuvering, Ethan and the aquarium moved into a college apartment with Joe.

At first Joe wasn't sure about sharing their limited living space with a tank full of stinky fish, but when the occasional female visitor gushed over their colorful living room decor, he acted as if setting up the aquarium had been his idea alone.

Ethan loved that aquarium. Was he one lucky guy or what? He couldn't have been happier.

I first met 28-year-old Ethan on evening hospital rounds. Right away I knew he was a different sort of soul.

Six-foot-two inches, blue-eyed and tanned-bodied, Ethan sat perfectly erect and uncomplaining in his hospital bed, calmly flipping through a months-old *Sports Illustrated* while a rosy-cheeked, serious-faced little girl rolled every hair on his head in pink sponge curlers. His wife, Jenny, mother of the talented four-year-old stylist, dozed in a chair next to the bed.

Hairstyle completed, Ethan agreed with his daughter, April, that he did indeed look *very* pretty. I *think* I saw him hesitate for just a moment before cheerfully allowing her to paint his toenails a shocking shade of purple. He enjoyed his relationship with April, and was a willing partner in play, even if "beauty shop" wasn't his favorite game.

Ethan loved that little girl. Was he one lucky guy or what? He couldn't have been happier.

Though he had had diabetes for more than ten years, Ethan didn't look sick. He took good care of himself. He followed his diet, never allowing himself to consume even a smidgen of anything sweet. He exercised regularly, diligently monitored his blood sugar, and carefully injected himself with insulin four times a day.

Diabetes is a serious disease for which as yet there is no cure. The disease can and does affect every system in the body. The damage it causes may be noticed immediately, or it may be delayed for months or even years. Sadly, there will always be some damage.

In Ethan's case, both eyes were affected. Shortly after entering college, he was unable to pass the visual test necessary to renew his driver's license. That wasn't too bad since he had always loved to bicycle, and his bike could take him just about anywhere he wanted to go. He was able to finish college and graduated in the top third of his class. He was immediately hired by a good company.

Ethan loved his new job. Was he one lucky guy or what? He couldn't have been happier.

Though his eyesight was bad, public transportation afforded Ethan the mobility he needed to work in the city. For several years he managed well, making only slight lifestyle modifications to help him cope with his failing vision.

Lately, though, things were getting worse. In a short period of time, Ethan went from dealing with poor vision to almost total blindness.

I felt terribly sorry for Ethan. He was too young to be facing such a serious complication. The future did not look good for this lighthearted young father.

Ethan, always an optimist, had another opinion.

Each time I entered his room, Ethan had a funny story or a joke for me. Sometimes he sang a goofy song or recited a silly poem. I would go home at the end of my shift, repeat the day's humorous tale, and have my family in stitches.

Nurses tend to label such behavior in their patients "denial." Ethan, however, wasn't in denial. He understood, accepted, and dealt with his situation in an unusually positive manner.

One morning when I delivered Ethan's morning insulin injection to his bedside, I found him grinning from ear to ear. He was practically jumping up and down in the hospital bed. I wasn't going to believe what had just happened to him. This was *great* news. The *best* news.

Only moments before, he had correctly answered a trivia question on the radio. He had won a prize! A terrific prize!

And what would the prize be? Perhaps a CD collection?

No.

Tickets to a concert?

No.

A trip?

No.

What then?

Doughnuts! A dozen doughnuts! A *really* great prize!

Doughnuts—for a diabetic. For a diabetic who followed his diet so diligently he wouldn't dream of eating *even a smidgen* of anything sweet.

Ethan loved winning those doughnuts. Was he one lucky guy or what? He couldn't have been happier.

Ethan and I were buddies for just one week. Once his diabetes was stabilized, he was discharged from the hospital and our paths never crossed again. I remember him well and I often wonder how he is faring. One thing I know—looking back on his life and the way he lived it, I have to agree: *Ethan, you are one lucky guy.*

A man's spirit sustains him in sickness.

—PROVERBS 18:14

CHAPTER THIRTY-TWO

With Our Shoes On

*H*ome health nursing has allowed me to get to know my patients in their most familiar of environments, doing what they value and enjoy the most. Home nursing is a relaxed, relatively low-stress type of nursing. However, even in this setting, the unexpected can happen.

❧ ❧ ❧

Preacher Owens lived on a narrow gravel street in an older section of my town. Many of the houses on his street had a sagging couch on the front porch, most had a sagging dog or two asleep on the front stoop, and almost all had a couple of sagging old women gossiping in the side yards. The neighborhood, like its residents, had seen better days. Most of the folks, like the houses they lived in, were a bit leaky and creaky and needed a few of their moving parts replaced.

It was only when he refused to eat—refused to eat another bite of "that awful hospital food"—that Dr. Keys, against his better judgment, released Preacher Owens to go home. The preacher had been hospitalized five days earlier and was recovering from a nasty kidney infection. He was still very weak, running a low-grade fever, and complaining of pain in his back. However, if he rested, drank plenty of fluids, and—most importantly—took every single dose of his prescribed antibiotics, he would probably recover from the infection. To help ensure that Preacher Owens would comply with his medical orders, and to monitor his progress, Dr. Keys requested that I check on the patient daily for the next two weeks.

Thelma, Preacher Owens' niece, greeted me on the front porch with a grandmotherly hug and a kiss on the cheek. She was dressed in a bright flowered housedress and smelled pleasantly of an appealing combination of Ivory Soap, Pine Sol, and fried chicken.

"I'm real glad that you come to check on my uncle, because he sure does need checking on."

Preacher Owens was less than enthused at my intrusion onto his property. He nodded in my direction but would not be distracted from the job at hand. Lined up in front of the straightback chair in which he sat were seven pairs of shoes and boots. Methodically he was polishing each pair until he could see his face in the shine.

Detailing seven pairs of shoes like that takes a good long while. I was already on my second glass of iced tea, graciously prepared by niece Thelma, when the preacher leaned back in his chair and grudgingly allowed me to take his blood pressure and temperature.

Once I convinced him I was there to make sure he didn't have to go back to the hospital rather than sending him there—in fact, I didn't even work for the hospital—and once I agreed that hospital food does indeed have a "whang" to it, he warmed up to me a bit.

As I examined Preacher Owens, he told me he had been shining his shoes for church when he had collapsed and had to be taken to the hospital. He wasn't called Preacher Owens without cause. At 88 years of age, he still served a vibrant little church and delivered two sermons every Sunday. I marveled at his dedication, tentatively asked for a urine specimen, and placed his antibiotics in a seven-day pill box. By the time my visit was over, I felt I had won his affection. He certainly had mine.

The next day I was concerned when Preacher Owens did not answer his locked door. I knocked and knocked, jiggled the doorknob, and searched the perimeter of the tiny house for an open window. Finally I phoned Thelma, but the preacher had never agreed to let her keep a spare key to his house. Reluctantly I summoned the police. I prayed that the preacher was sleeping soundly, had neglected to put his hearing aids in, or was just acting ornery and not answering his door.

My eyes teared up when I entered the house, followed by a nervous policeman, and found Preacher Owens in his recliner. He was wearing a pair of freshly polished black wingtips. His Bible was open in his lap and Sunday's sermon notes had been completed. The preacher was not resting in physical sleep as I had hoped, but he had certainly been granted rest from his life's work.

Thelma, her three grown daughters, two of her grandsons, Preacher Owens' six brothers-in-law, and numerous neighbors seemed to appear from nowhere. I gave them the sad news. They and several of the preacher's church members congregated in small groups in the yard. I heard comforting murmurs of condolences spoken in hushed tones. Someone went inside to call for the undertaker, and Thelma brought out iced tea for the adults and red Kool-Aid for the children.

I was impressed by the quiet respect so evident in these people for their old friend.

I was not impressed by the sight of the undertaker.

He slid out of a dusty, beat-up-looking station wagon-turned-hearse. The man wore a purple-and-turquoise wind suit, a gold ring on every finger, and at least a dozen gold chains around his neck. He looked cheesy to me—nothing like the sedate, gray-suited funeral directors I was accustomed to seeing. I stood back while he and his assistant placed the body onto the stretcher. The crowd in the yard parted like the Red Sea and stood respectfully as the undertaker and his helper loaded Preacher Owens into the back of the hearse.

I said nothing but secretly fumed: *What a disgrace for the body of such a dignified, godly man to be tended to by such a disrespectful-looking man as this!*

After the doors of the hearse were slammed shut, the flamboyantly dressed driver walked back to the crowd, now numbering more than 30. I assumed he wanted to know who was in charge here, or, more accurately, exactly who was going to pay for his services.

I was humbled and speechless when instead he asked us to join him in prayer. We formed a circle, and then at his leading, right there in the yard, we knelt down on our respective knees. In the most gentle, soft, and tender voice this man, looking more like a low-budget lounge singer than a psalmist, began to speak a fervent, heartfelt prayer, thanking the Lord for Preacher Owens, for his influence in the community and in the church, and for a peaceful end to a life well lived. He ended his prayer with these words:

> May each of us,
> when it comes our time to die, Lord,
> meet You as did Preacher Owens,
> with our shoes shined and ready to go.
> Amen.

Behold, a man stood before me in bright clothing.

—ACTS 10:30 KJV

CHAPTER THIRTY-THREE

Hard Hat and Texas Hair

Though I encounter lots of sad situations and confront tragedy on almost a daily basis, I also witness some hilarious moments. Laughter is healing, and while working as an industrial nurse with a bunch of rough, tough men, I experienced great healing.

❧ ❧ ❧

When my children were preschoolers, I was always on the lookout for part-time nursing positions that would pay well but still fit in with my desire to be mostly a mom. The ad in a nearby town's newspaper was intriguing:

> *Wanted: Registered Nurse*
> *for part-time work.*
> *Flexible hours, casual working environment.*
> *Call for interview.*

I phoned for information and was told that the position was for a nurse to work in a plant that manufactured ceramics. Since I had done some ceramics once myself (a lovely canister set and a pair of Christmas angels) I felt I knew something about ceramics. Still, I really couldn't understand why a ceramic shop would need a nurse. But with nothing to lose, I went ahead and scheduled an interview.

I dressed carefully, made sure my nursing license and my Social Security card were in my purse, and checked my hair—I was wearing infamous Big Texas Hair at the time— before leaving the house. I drove the 20 miles to the community where the plant was located, and then followed the directions I had been given over the phone. I was surprised to find that the shop would be located so far out of town. Just how much business could they receive at such an out of-the-way location?

Upon arrival at the plant, I quickly realized that there is more than one kind of "ceramics." There are the Christmas-angel-type ceramics, and then there are the industrial-type ceramics—in other words, bricks! This "ceramic factory" turned out to be a brick-making plant in need of an industrial nurse.

I was hired on the spot. (Later I learned I had been the only applicant.) I was happy to discover that I wouldn't have to wear a uniform. Even blue jeans would be fine. However, my joy was somewhat tempered when I was issued steel-toed boots and a hard hat. A hard hat and big hair just don't mix, and my mass of well-sprayed curls was soon reduced to a sticky, sweaty, helmet-shaped mess on my head.

As we toured the plant, I realized my boots were heavy and at least two sizes too large. The plant manager was so long-legged I had to frequently break into a clompety-clomp jog to keep up with his stride. And I wanted to keep up, because if I got left behind, I wasn't sure I would ever find my way out.

The plant consisted of several huge, dust-filled metal buildings filled with enormous, noisy, angry-looking machines. The floor was concrete with white markings (indicating forklift routes) and yellow markings (indicating safe areas in which to walk).

I had been hired to promote safety and to provide first aid. Worker's comp claims had been high the past two years, and it was hoped that my presence would provide a liaison between labor and management, with a resulting reduction of claims. I would also be responsible for maintaining employee health records and for conducting monthly health-and-safety meetings.

I believed it was most important to quickly get to know the people I would serve. Until now my patients had been mostly cheerful young mothers, chubby-cheeked children, and toothless old men. This group did not fall into any of those familiar categories.

The plant employed 63 men. The employees were blue-collar workers and most had a high-school education or less. The working conditions at the plant were rugged, the hours were long, and the wages poor. The men who worked there did so because of necessity, not out of choice.

I promptly scheduled the men for a blood pressure check, knowing that the taking of blood pressures would give me a moment with each employee individually. The men would have a chance to meet me, and perhaps I would learn a few of their names and maybe even get to know some of them.

The workers came to my office (also called "the infirmary") in groups of ten. A few of the men leered at me, but most of them just eyed me suspiciously. I think they all wondered if I was really one of them or just another management-type person sent to harass them. A few seemed generally friendly. I checked their blood pressures, and a couple of times my own blood pressure went up at the detailed anatomical drawings artistically tattooed on their arms.

I continued to work at the brick plant a few hours a week. Gradually some of the men began to trust me. I bandaged their cuts, wrapped their sore elbows, and gave them flu shots. We had a blood drive and a canned food drive, and we took up a collection when a worker's house burned down.

In time I began to see past their coarse language and dirty fingernails, and some of them began to overlook my education and my unreasonable insistence that they wipe their feet at the infirmary door.

I asked about their children and remembered their birthdays. They told me of their efforts to save for a house and questioned me about their learning-disabled kids.

With as much progress as I hoped I had made, I was still less than thrilled when the plant manager asked me to talk to the workers about AIDS at the next health-and-safety meeting. I was fine talking to them about heat stroke and athlete's foot. I had even dealt with the dicey subject of jock itch. But talk to 63 rough, tough, hard-drinking, party-loving men about a sexually transmitted disease? No, I was not thrilled with the idea. But I had a job to carry out, and I could ill afford to mess it up.

I did my research, obtained some handout literature from the state health department, and prepared myself for the inevitable snickers and dreaded innuendos I was sure would accompany my talk.

On the day of the meeting, the men gathered in the break room. I gave them the most basic of information about the HIV virus, how it is transmitted, how they could keep from getting the virus, and where they could get tested if they felt they might already have been exposed.

I spoke in greater detail about protecting themselves at work. Someone was always getting cut or scraped, and since I was only on duty a few hours a week, they often took care of each other. Usually these incidents were minor, but occasionally a serious accident occurred. They needed to avoid blood exposure when providing first aid to an injured coworker. I told them that I had placed latex gloves in convenient locations throughout the plant and that they were to use them to avoid exposing themselves to potentially infected blood.

I stressed that they must not get any blood, other than their own, on their skin.

I paused to take a breath and realized that the room was so quiet one could have heard a pin drop. The group had scarcely moved since I had begun talking. Tentatively I asked if anyone had a question.

One hand went up. I cringed inside. The hand belonged to a notorious rabble-rouser. Now *rabble* wasn't *exactly* what the other men said he raised, but I believe I make my point.

"Yes, Hank?" I acknowledged him, noting his serious expression, but preparing for the worst.

"Uh, ma'am . . . can I get AIDS from cleaning fish?"

When the tension is thick and the subject is tough, laughter is usually the best kind of medicine!

Our mouths were filled with laughter.

—PSALM 126:2

CHAPTER THIRTY-FOUR

Behind Closed Doors

*H*ospitals are staffed by a variety of professionals: doctors, nurses, lab and radiology technicians, respiratory and physical therapists. All of these workers contribute to the overall care of ill or injured patients.

There is another group of often-unnoticed folks whose roles, though easily overlooked, are vital to the smooth functioning of a busy health-care facility. This group has a special place in my heart.

❧ ❧ ❧

My friend Ricky is a busy man.

He and I work at the hospital together. Ricky doesn't come in on Tuesdays. Last week I teased him about his cushy four-day work schedule, but he stopped me short.

"Tuesday is not really my day off."

I learned that on his one morning away from the hospital, Ricky works in his church's office. He answers the phone, files, and straightens. In the afternoon he travels across town to an elementary school, where he tutors children who need extra help with their reading skills.

So much for Ricky slacking off.

✍ ✍ ✍

Trying to wake up, I begin my hospital shift at the coffeepot.

Full of energy, Ricky starts his workday at a dead run, barely slowed by a limp.

I cover the medical-surgical unit of the hospital.

Ricky's assignment includes the whole facility: central supply, dietary, medical records, medical-surgical, ER, ICU, and maintenance. They all expect Ricky to come when they call.

I accumulate sick time and vacation time. The hospital provides me with health insurance, and I receive a fairly generous biweekly paycheck.

Ricky receives gold-plated "hours of service" pins and appreciative pats on the back—but no money.

Ricky's mom good-naturedly complains that he likes volunteering at the hospital so much she's surprised he doesn't pack his pajamas and stay all night. Ricky is so helpful and cheerful that if he *did* decide to sleep over the night-shift workers would be delighted. But I'm afraid Ricky wouldn't get much sleep; someone would be sure to find something for him to do.

I think Ricky makes such a good volunteer because he knows hospitals. In his 40-plus years, Ricky has been what nurses call a "repeat customer," a "frequent flyer." When he was ten, he contracted encephalitis and lay unresponsive for more than a month. His mom says his survival was a miracle, but Ricky just shrugs. Some years later, while a teenager, Ricky was involved in a car accident. Treatment of his injuries included surgery on both legs. The illness and accident left Ricky with a few problems, but he gets along okay.

It was during one of those lengthy hospital stays that typically good-natured Ricky became unhappy.

"What's the problem?" his mom asked. "The food?"

"No." The hospital food was pretty good.

"The nurses?"

"No." The nurses were friendly and pretty.

Was it the TV? The bed?

"No." The room's TV reception was clear and the electric controls on the bed worked fine.

"What then?"

"*Prissy.*" His dog. He missed her. Could she come to visit him? "*Please?*"

A dog? In a hospital?

"I don't *think* so," declared the head nurse.

"No way!" exclaimed the infection control officer.

"We would *never* consider it," spoke the unit's manager.

So Ricky's mother, a calm, nonconfrontational, rule-keeping woman, did what any mother in her situation would do.

She sneaked Prissy up the stairs and into Ricky's room. Several times. Prissy was small, did not smell or shed, and was neither a drooler nor a barker. Ricky's mother's carefully crafted canine sneaks were carried off without a hitch—except for one close call when she took the elevator instead of the stairs. The sleeve of the raincoat Prissy was wrapped in began to wag gaily. But luckily none of the other passengers noticed.

Each time Ricky's mom brought her to the hospital, Prissy was overjoyed to see her best pal Ricky. Where had he been? When was he coming home?

With the door to his room shut, Ricky and Prissy enjoyed playful visits in his hospital bed. Whenever Ricky heard someone at his door, he threw the covers over Prissy and pretended to be asleep. She seemed to understand the clandestine nature of her visits, because she held still under the blankets.

Only once did they get caught.

Ricky and Prissy were resting in bed watching Gilligan's Island. The TV was turned up loud, and Ricky didn't hear the nurse until she was in the room, standing at his bedside.

Prissy looked at the nurse.

The nurse looked at Prissy.

Prissy's tale began to wag. Just a bit.

The nurse began to smile. Just a bit. Then, without saying a word, she turned around, walked from the room, and closed the door behind her.

She told no one.

My friend Ricky is at the hospital tonight—not working, but in his pajamas. Last week he fell and fractured his kneecap. He had surgery and is already working with a physical therapist to get back on his feet and return to work. He has to. We need him.

I need him.

I need Ricky around to remind me that work is supposed to be fun and to help me remember that money isn't the only reason to do a good job. I need my friend Ricky to regularly show me that happiness comes from who you are inside, not what you appear to be on the outside.

I've been checking in on Ricky in his hospital room frequently since his accident. He likes company and I want to be sure he's all right.

But I know to be careful about one thing: I never forget to knock before I open Ricky's door.

Your work will be rewarded.

—2 CHRONICLES 15:7

CHAPTER THIRTY-FIVE

Till the Cats Come Home

The story of a pet from the past illustrated to me the unexplainable need that folks have to return to their roots—to somehow, some way get home.

ℐ♥ ℐ♥ ℐ♥

The problem started with one innocent, sweet, fluffy white kitty. They had never had pets; on the farm, animals were kept only for their usefulness. It took days of begging from all four children to get their daddy, James, to consent to let them adopt the little ball of fur. Though keeping the kitten went against his better judgment, James figured a cat *would* help keep the mouse population down, so he consented to let them keep the little stray. But it would live in the barn, not the house.

Miss Kitty, as the children's new pet was called, turned out to be a very romantic soul, and within a few short months she presented the family with eight additional baby mouse-catchers. When the kittens were weaned, all but two were easily given away to nearby neighbors. The two leftover cats took after their mother, and within a few short months they too produced kittens. This time most, but not all, of the babies found homes. The ones that didn't grew up and created families of their own.

Pretty soon things got out of hand. All the neighbors who had wanted cats now had plenty, and James found it nearly impossible to find a home for an unwanted kitten.

The novelty of having a cat had long since worn off for the children and they rarely even played with Miss Kitty, much less with any of her children or grandchildren. James had to remind them every day to feed and water the cats, and they argued annoyingly over whose turn it was. The barn became so overrun with meowing felines that James couldn't get any work done for tripping over tall tails and stepping on furry feet.

Finally he had had it. This was a farm, not a cat house. The cats had to go. The cats *were going*. All of them.

Ray, at 12 years old, was the eldest of the children. Daddy gave him the job of disposing of the cats. Ray was to take them out into the woods, and, employing a rural animal control solution that, sadly, was a common one in those days, shoot them—all 13 of them.

Ray had heard older boys at school bragging about wild escapades involving shooting stray cats, so figured it would be fun to kill them. Shooting 13 cats—now that would be something to brag about to his friends!

It wasn't.

It took almost an hour for Ray to locate Miss Kitty, but he finally found her and her descendants asleep in a far corner of the barn. Not only was Miss Kitty's family cranky at having their naps disturbed, but they weren't at all happy about being dropped without ceremony into a burlap feed sack. When Ray picked them up, they yowled in great protest, but once in the bag they grew silent and still. When he had caught all 13 of them, Ray set out for the woods. He carried the heavy sack in one hand and his daddy's rifle in the other, and he hiked a good half-hour, deep into the forest before stopping.

Ray's plan was to shoot one cat at a time. It just happened that Miss Kitty was at the top of the sack's heap, so he pulled her out first. Ray had expected the cats to be so afraid of him that, once out of the sack, they would tear out running through the woods. He would take aim, fire, and (expert marksman that he believed he was) hit his target just before it scampered out of the rifle's range.

Miss Kitty did not cooperate. She was so happy to be out of the stuffy sack she did everything she could to show Ray her gratitude. She rubbed back and forth against his legs. She purred her prettiest purr in her loudest voice. She looked up at him with big blue eyes full of adoration. She sprawled across his feet.

Ray tried to chase her away. He yelled. He called her ugly names. He clapped his hands and stomped his feet.

Miss Kitty didn't budge from her place at his feet and even seemed to smile a kitty cat smile at him.

No problem. Ray decided he would save her for later and start with one of the other cats. He stuffed Miss Kitty back into the sack and pulled out one of her grandchildren.

But the same thing happened. The grateful-to-be-freed kitten rubbed and purred against him. It wouldn't even consider walking away, much less running from him.

By now Ray was frustrated. What had sounded like fun wasn't so much fun anymore. He tried again and again, but no matter which cat came out of the bag, it did so ready to prove its love and devotion to him. He even tried running away from one of the cats, but it just scampered happily along after him.

Finally Ray gave up. He tied the top of the sack closed and reluctantly threw it and its squirmy contents right into the creek.

Ray was tired and miserable when he returned home. Daddy asked him if he had taken care of the problem. He nodded and was grateful not to be asked for details.

No one was more surprised and no one was more relieved than Ray was when, the next evening after supper, he looked out and saw Miss Kitty and her 12 relatives trotting back into the yard. Their fur was muddy and matted but their tails were held high.

It was good to be home.

Ray was surprised and happy when Daddy didn't ask questions, but he sure had some of his own. Those questions were answered when he returned to the creek and found the sack where it had caught on a tree branch and saw the ragged hole the cats had chewed through it.

James held his tongue regarding the mystical resurrection of Miss Kitty and her family, but still wishing to be rid of the animals, on his next trip to town he loaded the 13 cats into a box and put the box in the trunk of the car. About 12 miles away from the farm he pulled over, stopped the car, got out, and opened the trunk. He took the box of cats out, set it down on the grass beside the road, and loosened the lid. Then he quickly got back into his car and sped away.

The deed was done.

The problem was solved.

No more cats.

He thought.

One week later James was working in the barn when he felt something rub against his leg. He looked down.

It couldn't be.

It was.

Miss Kitty had returned. So had the others. All 12 of them. They were ragged, weak, skinny, and scarred.

It was good to be home.

James was a basically kind man, but he had never been a sentimental man. Just as he had tried to teach Ray, James had learned from his daddy that an animal was just an animal.

That teaching came to an end the day the cats came home. When James saw that Miss Kitty was limping and when he found that her paws were bloody and sore, it got to him.

That afternoon he called Ray aside and gruffly told him he had given up. If Miss Kitty and the rest of those cats wanted to come home that badly, he wasn't going to try to get rid of them. They could stay around for as long as they wanted.

James was a patient of mine. During his illness I visited his house twice a week. He was a large, gentle man and he had wonderful twinkling eyes. When he told me this story, those sparkly eyes teared up when he remembered discovering Miss Kitty's bleeding paws. Even though 40 years had passed since the memorable feline return, he was still moved to remember what a bunch of cats had gone through to come home.

James wisely advised me to remember that those cats weren't so different than people. There is something in nature that calls all living creatures home.

When I greet my beloved family at the end of each long day, I'm glad that's so.

And they returned home.

—ACTS 21:6

CHAPTER THIRTY-SIX

Staying Warm

*M*y mother, packing for an upcoming medical mission trip, recently learned some lessons about generosity. While watching her, I learned some of the same lessons myself.

❧ ❧ ❧

Rosa checked the satchel with care. She had packed corn tortillas tightly wrapped in paper, plastic bags of beans and rice, and two dozen apples. Alicia, her youngest, had chosen the largest, firmest, best-looking apples left on the trees. Good weather had blessed the mountain this year, and branches of the family's eight apple trees hung heavy with fruit.

Rosa's face revealed the mixed emotions she felt today. As he did every fall, her husband, Antonio, would leave the village and travel to Mexico City, where he would live and work during the winter months. She was grateful for the money he would earn and send home, though reluctant as always to see him go.

This year's departure was made much harder because her oldest son, Thomas, age 12, would be making the trip for the first time in his life. The boy and his dad would walk the two-day journey to reach the highway. There they would catch the bus into Mexico City. Rosa knew Thomas was excited. He was proud to be a man, to be old enough to go off to seek work with Papa, to help the family. He was eager to see the city he had heard so much about.

She would miss him.

Antonio and Thomas had been gone four days when Rosa was first startled, then frightened to see Thomas trudging alone up the steep hill toward the family's compound. She ran to meet him, sure Antonio had been hurt or was sick, and had sent Thomas to get help.

Thomas stood stiffly, not returning his mother's embrace, and at first he could not find a voice to answer her rapid questions. Finally, wearily, flatly, he told his mother of the past four days.

Papa was not hurt or sick. He was gone.

Gone?

Papa had boarded the bus to Mexico City and disappeared in a cloud of diesel-fumed dust. Only a moment before, Thomas had stood ready to step onto the bus behind his papa. He was confused when at the last possible second his papa pushed him away and spoke in a strange voice.

"You are older now, ready to be the man of the family. You are not going to the city with me, but back home to your mother and sisters. Tell them I am not coming back."

The boy had stood stunned as he watched the bus disappear. Then had begun to sob and stumble toward home. He hadn't felt like a man at all.

On the last day of a recent medical mission trip to Mexico, we mission workers discovered that the drive from the hotel to the village where we were to work was longer than we had expected. We also found the number and needs of the village residents to be greater than we had anticipated. It was decided that the medical team would spend the night on the mountain rather than return to the hotel. We would stay in the homes of the local folks so we could work a bit longer and finish up before beginning the long trip home the next day.

My mother and I, along with my friends Elsa and Toni, were assigned to stay together in the home of Rosa. She and her three youngest children lived in a tidy compound with a kitchen, a separate sleeping house, and an outhouse. They also had a pig and several chickens.

It was well past nightfall when we entered the compound where Rosa lived. She greeted us warmly and motioned for us to enter her cozy kitchen. She served us coffee and potatoes fried with onions and jalapenos. We warmed our hands over the open fire she used for cooking and chatted with her about her family.

Rosa told us the story of her husband's departure. For months she had watched and waited for his return. Surely there had been a mistake. He would come home. She knew it.

Sadly, though, Antonio kept his last words to the boy. Seven years had passed and she had not seen or heard from him.

The family survived that first year and those that followed by eating apples—apples for breakfast and apples for supper. It had been hard, and often they were hungry.

But things were better now. Thomas and his sister, at ages 17 and 19, were considered grown, old enough to live and work in the city. They sent home money regularly to their mother and younger sisters. At least now they always had plenty to eat.

After our tasty meal, we began to yawn. Rosa showed us to the sleeping hut. Its clean-swept dirt floor held two double beds. She and her girls would stay with a neighbor tonight. We would have the room to ourselves.

A sweet aroma filled the hut. We saw that ripe apples were stored in every available space. Apples were layered under the beds, stacked on shelves, heaped in boxes. Never had I seen so many apples. Like a fragrant hedge against future hunger, the stored apples represented security for the family.

Mom, Toni, Elsa, and I talked late into the night, then drifted off to sleep one by one. The apples under our beds gave off a heavenly aroma and we slept well, enjoying the sweetest of dreams.

The next morning we packed our belongings and made our beds. It is our custom, in response to such hospitality, to leave behind small tokens of our gratitude. We placed our offerings on one of the beds. Toni left a pretty bandanna, Elsa a Bible story book for Rosa's girls, and Mom a bottle of hand lotion. I added two chocolate bars to the collection.

We gathered our things and prepared to leave. Impulsively Mom pulled off her navy blue parka, folded it neatly, and placed it next to the stack of gifts. It was very cold here on the mountain, and she had noticed that our hostess wore only a thin and tattered sweater. In just a few hours we would be traveling to the warmer valley. She shivered but assured us she could manage just fine without a coat for the next few hours.

Later that winter Mom and I were chatting as she packed for another mission trip. She lamented the loss of the navy blue parka. It had fit her just right, did not show dirt, and was so lightweight it could be rolled up tightly and shoved into an already-stuffed-to-the-brim bag. It had been perfect for travel. A part of her even wished she still had it, especially for this trip. She sort of wished she hadn't given it away.

"Mom," I asked, " have you been cold a single time since you gave that coat away?"

"No," she mused, "I have to say I haven't been really cold even once this winter." She tucked a plaid jacket into her bag. It fit perfectly.

"But," she continued with a smile, "I *have* had this constant, *crazy* craving for apples."

> *The man with two tunics should share*
> *with him who has none.*
>
> —LUKE 3:11

CHAPTER THIRTY-SEVEN

New Sandals for Grandma

Some of my best nursing instructors have been folks with no medical training at all. From these teachers I have learned to care for the souls and the spirits of my patients, not just for their bodies.

❧ ❧ ❧

My mom called last week. She told me that my grandma, who lives in a nursing home, is doing much better. Though she has no medical training, Mom is an expert when it comes to Grandma's health. If she says Grandma is better, I believe her.

So this was the best of news. What has been going on with my 89-year-old grandma? Has she been able to take a few steps without her wheelchair? Did the doctor finally get her arthritis medication adjusted? Is her blood pressure down?

Well, no, not exactly. She remains confined to her wheelchair and still complains of arthritic pain, and her blood pressure is still way too high.

But she's better?

Yes.

How can you tell?

Grandma asked for sandals. New ones. Navy blue. With a medium heel. And a new handbag to match.

Mom is right. Though this particularly peculiar phenomenon has never been written up in the medical journals, a sudden feeling of discontent with one's current wardrobe accompanied by a strong urge to buy something new to wear to church is definitely a sign of improved health and well-being.

At least with Grandma.

As time passes, we realize Grandma's health is becoming increasingly fragile. She has days when she feels poorly and isn't herself. Sometimes the difficult days stretch into difficult weeks. When she feels bad, Grandma tends to focus almost exclusively on her aches and pains, her meals and her snacks, and what time she's to get her bath. She will display little regard for the very topics she would normally find most interesting—topics such as the great-grandchildren, unexpected changes in the weather, and the latest juicy nursing home gossip.

Just about the time we determine to accept these changes in Grandma's outlook as yet another of the inevitable symptoms of aging (after all, she *is* 89 years old), she'll snap out of it.

Grandma will wake up one morning feeling a bit better. We'll notice that her short-term memory is sharper, her conversation more animated, and her wardrobe *most inadequate.*

In another day or two Grandma will begin to feel a lot better. The day's menu will pale in importance next to her immediate need for a new half-slip. Concerns about her arthritis will be put aside in the quest for a white pleated skirt. Even an unexpected change in the nursing home's bath schedule becomes inconsequential when Grandma realizes she has *nothing* to wear on Sunday.

It isn't absolutely clear which comes first—the desire for new clothes or the improvement in Grandma's frame of mind. The two just seem to go together. However, Mom's response to Grandma's wardrobe request is always very clear: The woman goes shopping!

Grandma was wearing her new navy sandals. I told her how nice they looked on her and how much I liked her new handbag. I also commented on how good she looked and asked how she had been feeling lately.

"Annette, sometimes I just don't feel good," she told me. "My arthritis hurts me and I get tired of sitting in this old chair. But you know," she wriggled her toes in her new sandals, "your mother always seems to know just what I need to feel better."

"By the way, Hon, isn't that a new outfit you're wearing?" Grandma asked.

I sipped my coffee, crossed my legs, and smoothed the folds of my denim dress.

I had been down in the dumps for a couple of weeks. Nothing was seriously wrong; I had just been plagued with a bad case of the no-reason-at-all-to-feel-down-but-I-do blues. But today I noticed *I was feeling better.* At Grandma's question I smiled.

Upon my arrival the evening before, Mom had made a quick assessment of my cloudy mood and insisted we dash right down to a dress shop she knew was having a great sale. We had only an hour to shop before closing time, but if we hurried we could make it. We arrived before the shop closed, and at Mom's absolute insistence I bought the denim dress I was wearing. When Grandma posed her question, I realized I really hadn't needed anything new, but I just felt compelled to buy the new outfit.

You see, if I had passed it up, I would have gone against the most expert of medical advice. Somehow, Dr. Mom always knows just what Grandma and I need most!

She is clothed with strength and dignity;
she can laugh at the days to come.

—PROVERBS 31:25

CHAPTER THIRTY-EIGHT

Discharge Instructions

I take pride in the efficiency with which I do my work. I am very organized, and I complete my assigned tasks in a timely manner. I like to work extremely hard when I'm on the job, but I treasure my free time and enjoy spending time with my family. One evening, in my hurry to get home to my family, I missed out on some important information about Mr. Simmons.

✒ ✒ ✒

Today was Friday, and I was already thinking about the weekend. My husband, my two children, and I planned to participate in the annual Azalea Trails Fun Run in the nearby town of Tyler, Texas. My husband, Randy, is a sometimes runner, and I am at best a sporadic walker, but we had prepared for this annual event. We had done stretching exercises and made laps around the high-school track, and I had bought expensive new walking shoes. I was a bit prideful of my latest efforts to get into shape. *I deserved those fancy shoes,* and I wore them to work the week before the run to break them in.

The course would be beautiful, the weatherman predicted sunshine, and the event always proved to be well-organized. We would jog through neighborhoods of historic homes and admire the brilliant pink, red, and white azaleas lining the route. After the race we would enjoy a picnic lunch with other runners and applaud the winners in an outdoor awards ceremony. I couldn't wait for my hospital shift to end and the weekend to begin.

My workday was over. Finally. I was ready to go home, make my family a pre-race pasta supper, air out my new shoes, and go to bed early.

I had signed off my last chart and passed out my last pill, and I was fishing my keys from my purse when my coworker, Jill, asked me to help her finish up. She had received two admissions on her hall in the past hour and was running behind. Could I give Mr. Simmons his discharge instructions? He had been released to go home two hours before, but was waiting for a nurse to go over his packet of take-home information.

Jill is a good friend, but she is a slow mover. *If she were a little more organized like I am*, I fumed to myself, *she'd get off on time too*. I glanced at my watch and picked up Mr. Simmons' chart.

Having worked on the opposite hall all week, I had not seen or met any of Jill's patients. She tried to tell me something about his history, but I waved her away and told her I would just look at his chart. I saw that Mr. Simmons had been admitted with a heart attack, but because of his cardiologist's aggressive medical intervention his heart had sustained minimal damage. With careful adjustments to his lifestyle, Mr. Simmons could expect to live a comfortable, active life.

I hurried to room 208, my new shoes squeaking on the freshly buffed floor.

I shuffled through the packet of information: diet sheets . . . information on stress management . . . exercise instructions. Where to start? I found a checklist detailing topics I was to teach him.

"Let's see now, Mr. Simmons. Your doctor has recommended a low salt diet. You need to avoid salted snacks like nuts and chips, eat limited amounts of tomato products, use lots of fresh or frozen vegetables and . . . uh . . . avoid canned soups and fish. There are other foods to stay away from, but you can read about them in this pamphlet. Do you have any questions?"

"No, ma'am."

I handed him a hefty stack of diet sheets and marked through "Diet Teaching" on my checklist.

Great, I thought, *this won't take long.*

I turned to the next section in the packet. "Mr. Simmons, stress is very bad for your heart. You should learn to relax." I was on a roll, and I would be on my way home shortly. "You should practice deep-breathing exercises, and everyone should have a hobby. Hobbies that you enjoy can help reduce stress. Pets also promote relaxation. Do you have a pet, Mr. Simmons?"

"Yes, ma'am. I have a dog."

Another topic down. I drew a fat line through "Stress Management."

"Very good. Now let's talk about exercise." Almost done! I wiggled my toes in my new shoes. "When you have a heart condition, it is very important that you begin a regular exercise program. Do you exercise regularly?"

"No, ma'am."

"It is essential that you begin to exercise as soon as you get home. You should avoid exercising in the heat of the day, or you can exercise in an air-conditioned mall. If you experience chest pain or shortness of breath, then you should stop, rest, and take a nitroglycerin tablet. If you still have chest pain, then you should seek medical attention. Do you understand?"

"Yes, ma'am."

"Walking is the very best exercise there is. Anyone can do it. No matter how out of shape you may be, you can begin with a slow half-mile walk in your neighborhood." My mind drifted to the strenuous 5k walk I would complete in less than 24 hours. *I would probably finish in the first third. It felt good to be in shape again; what a shame that everyone can't see how important exercise is . . .*

"But, ma'am . . ."

"Mr. Simmons," I interrupted sternly, "there simply is no acceptable excuse. As I said, anyone can walk. You should begin with a half mile the first week, then gradually increase your distance until you are walking two miles, five times a week. You should continue this routine the rest of your life. It will get easier and easier. You might even learn to enjoy it. But you simply must walk."

"But, darlin'," protested Mr. Simmons as I happily crossed "Exercise" off my checklist: *"I ain't got no legs."*

Slowly, very slowly, I lowered my important checklist and raised my head to actually look into Mr. Simmons' sweet blue eyes. My gaze traveled the length of the hospital bed where he lay. The sheets were absolutely flat where his legs should have been. Mr. Simmons was a double amputee.

The fancy shoes I was wearing that day would provide support and protection for me on many journeys to come. They would take me from the mountains of Colorado to the beaches of Florida, with many stops in between. The greatest journey I would ever travel in those shoes, however, began with an arrogant stride into room 208 to provide instruction to a patient. As is so often the case, I, the teacher, became the student that day. A student in the school of slowing down. Of paying attention to *people*.

Thank you for a lesson well learned, Mr. Simmons. A lesson *very* well learned.

If anyone wants to be first,
he must be the very last,
and the servant of all.

—MARK 9:35

CHAPTER THIRTY-NINE

Trophies of My Own

I have received many rewards during my 18-year nursing career. Financially, I have been paid a good wage, and personally, nursing has provided the flexibility I needed to care for my husband and children. Of all the rewards I could list, however, I would count the greatest of all to be the privilege I have had to know and be loved by my patients.

❧ ❧ ❧

When my son, Russell, was five years old, I located a sturdy, barely used, maple bookcase at a secondhand furniture store. After I checked the price and found it would fit within my budget, I bought it. The shop owner helped me heave the heavy piece of furniture into the back of our family's station wagon, and I hauled it home.

The bookcase fit right into Russell's room and provided the perfect storage solution for his childhood treasures and clutter. He and I spent two afternoons arranging and rearranging some of his most valued possessions. After much discussion, we finally decided to put storybooks on the top shelf, art supplies on the middle shelf, and games and puzzles on the bottom.

Russell is grown now. His storybooks and games and puzzles were long ago relegated to the garage storeroom. When he was in high school he used the shelves to store his important stuff—an impressive collection of trophies, medals, and awards.

Russell is an accomplished athlete. A top-shelf row of shiny trophies attested to his abilities in football, basketball, and baseball. Various academic medals and ribbons, awarded for winning math and quiz bowl competitions, were displayed on the second shelf. The bottom shelf held plaques and mementos and a Christian leadership award he is especially proud of, bestowed on him at summer church camp.

Russell didn't brag, but he was proud of the accolades he received. I still am. The bits of wood and plaster and metal and glass I dusted each week represented my son's hard work, talent, and recognition.

I've never been awarded a trophy, a medal, a plaque, or a ribbon. I'm sure someone, somewhere, gives out a "Nurse of the Year" award, but I've never won it. I have, however, received my share of recognition. My patients and their families recognize me and reward me with hugs, smiles, and words of gratitude.

Many of them think *I'm it.*

I know because they tell me so.

Receiving love and affection is absolutely the best part of being a nurse and is more precious to me than any trophy or plaque. However, in a small cabinet in my living room I've collected and saved some tangible reminders of my patients' appreciation. I treasure this hodgepodge of beautiful, useful, and even curious items. They are of special meaning only to me because they are humble offerings of gratitude given to me by folks I love.

I do have a confession to make: A nurse is not supposed to take gifts from her patients. Doing so is considered, by some, to be unethical. I know I should protest when my patients thrust gifts into my hands, but I seldom do. The items they give to me are of great value to my heart, but of little value to my purse.

One of the shelves holds a white wicker basket stuffed full of cards and letters sent to me by patients and their families. When I'm feeling needy or blue, I take the basket down, make a cup of cocoa, and curl up in a comfortable chair. I sip, and read, and call to mind the folks who took the time to put their feelings into words. Most of the letters have been folded and unfolded so many times they're coming apart at the creases. Reading them always lifts my spirits.

Next to the basket is a three-dimensional, palm-sized Nativity scene. The holy setting, painstakingly rendered in plastic, canvas and yarn, is depicted in great detail. Mary, Joseph, the Christ child, and even the angels, wise men, and shepherds are all there. The elderly woman who crafted it has extremely poor vision, and I am deeply moved when I think of the time and work she spent making it for me.

Other emblems of devotion clutter the case. On a lower shelf, a delicate, rosebud-embellished, round porcelain box rests on an ivory-colored crocheted doily. Next to it is propped a plaque inscribed with an inspirational poem titled *What Is a Nurse?* A splintery wooden cross, with John 3:16 hand-carved in the center, occupies a place on the lower section of the display, and a set of three quilted pot holders sits next to it.

Some of my patients are gardeners, and I am the lucky recipient of gifts from their abundant harvests. Today my pantry holds two jars of homemade jelly and a bread bag full of shelled pecans. My freezer is stocked with a bag of tree-ripened peaches and one of garden-grown green beans.

In my yard, a fragrant blooming shrub reminds me of the man who, after presenting me with a newspaper-wrapped bouquet of gardenia blooms, gave me cuttings from the bush and showed me how to root them. Daffodils that come up in my yard every spring make me think of the woman who thinned her bed and gave me the gleanings. Their yellow color reminds me of her sunny disposition.

When I taste and smell and see these gifts, I am at once both humbled and grateful.

All of these items—the letters, the knickknacks, the food, and the flowers—are of little value to anyone but me. Some of them, I suppose, would likely even be scorned by yard sale patrons. But because of who and what they represent, they are dear to me.

I may never be awarded a plaque or a trophy, and I doubt I'll ever be crowned "queen of caregivers." Though I'm not likely to be issued a certificate for my abilities, I have just as truly received my rewards—*from the folks I've been blessed to know*.

When I remember the gifts I've been given, I think of Sam and Lily, Hope, Robert, and Mary. I remember Mrs. Jeffery and Preacher Owens, Sarah and Rosa and Ethan and Jeb. For in allowing me into their lives, these folks, as well as all the others who have crossed my path, have given me the best of all possible awards: They have given me the sacred privilege of knowing them and of hearing the stories of their hearts.

For them, and for their stories, I am grateful.

I thank my God
every time I remember you.

—PHILIPPIANS 1:3

✒ ✒ ✒

If you would like to write to Annette Smith,
find out about her other books, or
read her blog, please check out
www.annettesmithbooks.com

✒ ✒ ✒

More Helpful Books
from Harvest House Publishers

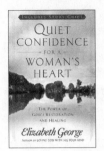

QUIET CONFIDENCE
FOR A WOMAN'S HEART
Elizabeth George

Take an gentle journey with bestselling author Elizabeth George and explore 12 life-changing truths God wants you to know. David, a man known for his great faith...and great failures... reveals how God gave him strength in the midst of challenges and peace in every situation. And God wants to do the same for you. Discover how He will...

- increase your joy through His loving kindness

- comfort you with the assurance that He's only a prayer away

- guide you with His wisdom when decisions must be made

You can count on God to help you live a life filled with faith, hope, and confidence. Includes questions for individual and group study.

SANITY SECRETS FOR
STRESSED-OUT WOMEN
Sue Augustine

Frustrated, frayed, frazzled, and fatigued—is that how you feel? Through biblical wisdom, research, and her own experiences, Sue Augustine's found and tested 25 ways to make life better balanced and more fulfilling. Going beyond the typical relaxation exercises for stress relief, Sue offers powerful tools to help you...

- recognize and deal with burnout

- recharge your body, mind, and spirit

- meet your needs so you can more effectively help others

Try these easy-to-implement lifestyle changes so you can experience more joy, contentment, and rest. You'll feel better and achieve more than you thought possible!

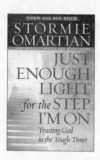

JUST ENOUGH LIGHT
FOR THE STEP I'M ON
Stormie Omartian

Do you wonder how you can get where you need to go in life and move into the purpose God has for you? During those times when the road ahead seems uncertain, take God's hand and let Him lead you. Discover how when you walk in His light you can

- overcome fear and doubt in difficult situations

- learn to see things from God's perspective

- trust that God will give you everything you need

Let this beautiful edition of *Just Enough Light for the Step I'm On* be a valuable tool in your devotional prayer life as you spend time every day with the One who knows where you need to go and how to get you there.

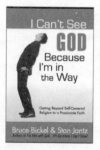

I CAN'T SEE GOD...
BECAUSE I'M IN THE WAY
Bruce Bickel and Stan Jantz

When you hear about Jesus' promise of an abundant life, do you think, *I'm a Christian, but I don't see God moving so abundantly in my life*. Could misconceptions be blocking your view of God? In this honest, personal, and occasionally humorous account of someone learning to see God more clearly, you'll discover that you too can...

- give up on religion and go for a relationship with God

- quit waiting for eternal life and start experiencing it now

- relax about finding God's will for your life

Could it be that you are your own worst enemy when it comes to realizing God's abundant life? Maybe it's time to change your spiritual perspective and experience God's presence in your life like never before.